Sonobeat Records

Sonobeat Records

• PIONEERING THE AUSTIN SOUND IN THE '60S •

RICKY STEIN

Charleston | London

THE
History
PRESS

Published by The History Press
Charleston, SC 29403
www.historypress.net

First published 2014

Manufactured in the United States

ISBN 978.1.62619.245.4

Library of Congress CIP data applied for.

For Em

Contents

Preface

I've had direct contact with Sonobeat Records all my life but did not find out about it until I started working as an intern for KLRU-TV in the summer of 2012. One day while waiting for further instruction on the set of *Austin City Limits*, I was lucky enough to strike up a conversation with Michael Emery, a longtime production assistant, camera operator, lighting designer, director and producer for the Austin PBS affiliate. He asked me about my career plans, and when I told him about my interest in musicology, he suggested I look up a website dedicated to a little-known local record label that played a key role in the development of the Austin music scene.

I was immediately interested, especially when I saw some of the names associated with the record label. There was Johnny Winter and Eric Johnson, Gary P. Nunn and Rusty Wier; but beyond the more famous names, there was Ernie Gammage listed as the composer of the first single of the Sonobeat discography. Ernie has been a close friend of my father, Rick Stein, for as long as I have been alive. My dad was a singer/songwriter in Austin in the 1970s. These were people he knew.

It sounded like an interesting and worthy project, but my time was limited between attending the University of Texas, working for KLRU and playing music around town. Fortunately, I was given the opportunity to write a senior thesis over the following two semesters on the topic of my choice. I suggested Sonobeat, and this project was born.

Over the next year, while finishing coursework at UT, contributing articles to the *Daily Texan*, playing gigs at the Hole in the Wall and trying to maintain some semblance of a social life, I managed to write a fifteen-thousand-word thesis titled "Home Lost and Found: Sonobeat Records and the Roots of the Austin Music Scene." I'd never written anything that long in my entire life, and when it was over, I decided I'd never do it again.

That was before Ernie put me in touch with The History Press. Ernie is a longtime family friend and longtime Austin musician. He's also a founding member of the Sweetarts, a local Austin band from the late 1960s whose single "A Picture of Me" was the first recording released by Sonobeat Records in 1967. Ernie told me about a publisher who might be interested in expanding my thesis into a book and asked me if I'd be interested.

Six months later, I've written my first manuscript, some thirty-two thousand words detailing the formation of the Austin music scene with this great little indie label as the focal point. As a native Austinite and second-generation Austin musician, I couldn't be happier with the subject matter. In researching this book, I've come to know some colorful personalities, engaging stories and a lot of great songs. I've learned a lot about my hometown and how this vibrant music scene that has been such an important part of my life came to be. Furthermore, I feel that I have shed some light on an almost-forgotten piece of Austin's past and hopefully given a little credit where it is due.

I hope the readers of this, my first, book get as much joy and satisfaction as I did writing it. It's a great, soulful city we live in, and I'm proud of all the places, things and, most of all, people who make it what it is. I hope this same spirit is reflected in the following pages.

Acknowledgements

As with virtually any work of this nature, there are countless individuals who have helped make this book happen. First off, I extend my thanks to Christen Thompson and The History Press for believing in this project. I am very grateful. An additional thank you goes to copyeditor Jaime Muehl for designing the pages and bringing the words to life.

Dr. Janet Davis headed our weekly thesis class at the University of Texas and was supportive from the very start. Her experience and advice taught me how to be a better researcher and writer. Similarly, Dr. Karl Miller served as thesis adviser and Dr. John Hoberman as second reader; I could not have asked for two more qualified, insightful and encouraging academic mentors to help me through the process.

In addition to introducing me to the story of Sonobeat Records in the first place, Michael Emery at KLRU served as a great resource throughout the project's early stages, suggesting key contacts and references that helped the idea take shape. Dr. Jason Mellard of Texas State took the time to meet me for coffee for several productive brainstorming sessions, and Kim Simpson, the Austin-based singer/songwriter, guitarist, author and radio host, was also extremely helpful in shaping my knowledge of the Austin music scene. John Wheat and everyone at the Dolph Briscoe Center for American History helped me locate documents and artifacts from the center's archives, including many of the original Sonobeat records themselves.

Bill Josey Jr. served as a primary source for this book, granting me an extended interview, as well as access to several of the images included herein, including the Sonobeat logo on the cover. He also took the time to review the manuscript on several occasions, correcting a few subtle and some not-so-subtle mistakes.

Ernie Gammage, Layton DePenning, John Inmon, Spencer Perkins, Mike Lucas, Jim Franklin, Wali King, Leonard Arnold, Ed Guinn and Tommy Taylor also granted me lengthy interviews that lent this work some critical firsthand perspective. Doug Hanners granted me an interview and also allowed me to use the tapes from his 1976 interviews with Bill Josey Sr., bringing the past back to life.

Michael Barnes of the *Austin American-Statesman* met me for coffee and suggested some contacts, all while broadening my cultural history of Austin and encouraging me to pursue this project. Thanks to his introduction, I was able to have a similar conversation with East Austin cultural expert Harold McMillan. Casey Monahan, Michael Corcoran, Eddie Wilson, Paul Drummond and Freddie Krc also provided helpful suggestions, clearing new pathways for research and analysis.

Finally, no list of acknowledgements would be complete without extending my deepest and utmost thanks to my friends, family and supporters who made this work not only possible but enjoyable as well. You've given me the biggest, best, most hospitable support group any writer or human being could ever ask for. I am extremely grateful. This book is for you.

Introduction

Austin, Texas. August 1968. The hot Texas sun blares down on the mostly empty streets slicing across downtown's main thoroughfare, South Congress Avenue. Shimmering in the heat, the 311-foot-tall granite dome of the Texas State Capitol still dominates the Austin skyline as it has since its construction in 1888; only recently has its superiority been challenged with the completion of the nearby Westgate Tower in 1967.

A handful of Ramblers and Cadillacs roll lazily down Congress in the Capital City of 234,000. The Texas legislature has ended session a little over a month ago and will not reconvene until next year; six blocks to the north, classes have not yet resumed at the other pillar of Austin culture, the University of Texas. The town is relatively quiet, especially in the business-dominated downtown area.

However, just seven blocks south of the Capitol on Congress Avenue, three musicians and a handful of friends are starting to make some noise. The setting: the newly opened Vulcan Gas Company. The music hall is spacious and mostly empty; though it is a popular alternative music venue by night, today it is being used as a makeshift recording studio in the heart of downtown Austin.

The players include drummer "Uncle John" Turner, bassist Tommy Shannon and a red-hot rising star in the Texas music scene, twenty-four-year-old albino blues guitarist and singer Johnny Winter. Together the group huddles around their amplifiers in the middle of the emptied-out hall trying to capture the energy of their incendiary live show that would soon make them national stars.

South Congress Avenue, October 1965. *PICA 02546. Austin History Center, Austin Public Library.*

In addition to the band, the people present during the session include Jim Franklin, the artist-in-residence at the Vulcan. A great fan and friend of the three musicians, he has taken the time to set up a swirling psychedelic light show to make the band feel relaxed and closer to a "live" setting. And off in the corner stand two men carefully adjusting the knobs and gauges on a custom-made portable recording console and Ampex 354 two-track recorder.

These two men, father and son Bill Josey Sr. and Jr., would go on to record dozens of local bands, musicians and singer/songwriters in Austin between the years 1967 and 1976, many of whom would go on to national prominence. In making these records, which the Joseys would release under the label "Sonobeat," the two music enthusiasts were able to capture the sounds of a budding musical mecca, a city that would proclaim itself the "Live Music Capital of the World" in the decades to come.

The story of Sonobeat Records is one that has seldom been told, its impact on Austin's famed music scene virtually completely overlooked.

An expansive commemorative website, a feature article in local music historian Doug Hanners's short-lived fanzine *Not Fade Away* and the occasional mention in various history books and dissertations composes the total published output regarding Sonobeat Records as of this writing. Yet the independent label played a huge part in bridging the gap between the psychedelic rock scene of the late 1960s and the progressive country movement that would soon follow.

Many aspiring Austin musicians drew inspiration from Austin's first nationally successful rock band, the infamous and iconic 13th Floor Elevators. Gradually, the rock-and-roll scene eventually shifted to country, and by the time Willie Nelson, Jerry Jeff Walker, Michael Martin Murphy and a cadre of other successful progressive country artists moved to Austin, the stage was set for the Capitol City's rise to national prominence. This history details the intermediary period, when the best of the local bands got their first taste of the recording business with a family-owned independent record label known as Sonobeat Records.

"Sonobeat had eclectic tastes and recorded acts that were both country and moving into progressive country," recalls Ernie Gammage, whose band the Sweetarts was one of the first groups recorded by Sonobeat. "Acts like Bill Wilson, Don Dean and Jim Chestnut, and even The Lavender Hill Express, had those leanings. I think one of the strengths of Sonobeat—and also its greatest weakness as a label—is that it was so eclectic. In that regard, it completely mirrored the music of Austin then…and now."

Today, the city of Austin is widely hailed as a cultural capital, internationally known for its sunny skies, friendly people and, most of all, its live music. Each spring, thousands of vans and tour buses line the downtown streets for South by Southwest; each fall, hundreds of thousands of music fans descend on Zilker Park to see some of the most popular acts in show business at the Austin City Limits Music Festival. Every night of the year, scores of bands play in dive bars scattered throughout town, and a couple dozen times per year Austin music is broadcast nationwide via the long-running PBS series *Austin City Limits*. When it comes to music, few towns come even close to the international renown that Austin has garnered without the major labels, publishing companies and media centers found in New York, Los Angeles, London and Nashville.

The fact that this "college town" of 800,000-plus citizens attained this high level of recognition in such a short amount of time demonstrates an unprecedented model for the growth of a music scene. Sonobeat Records played a key part in this transition. Unlike other major music centers,

Austin did not have any nationally recognized industry establishments that attracted hungry musicians across the country. Whereas New York, Los Angeles, London, Chicago, Memphis and Nashville made their names as musical hotbeds because of the studios and major labels that made them their headquarters, Austin's scene began with a much less commercial slant. Instead, it was the musicians themselves who formed the bedrock of what would become the world-renowned Austin music community.

Sonobeat Records had a short-lived tenure in Austin's musical history, producing twenty-four 45rpm singles, two commercial albums and seven noncommercial promotional/demo albums on its own label. Only two of the Sonobeat albums were ever picked up by nationally distributed labels. However, in that span of time, Sonobeat played a key role in discovering dozens of musicians and songwriters who would go on to have successful careers and play key roles in the development of the Austin music scene. This book will focus on the history of Sonobeat Records while comparing the development of the Austin music scene to that of other major music centers. In doing so, I hope to shed light on some of the characters, events and songs that led Austin to become the cultural capital that it is today.

A Brief History of Music in Austin Up to the 1960s

The history of Austin music starts with the saloons and music halls that arrived shortly after the small town of Waterloo was founded on the banks of the Colorado River in 1837. The newly formed Republic of Texas had just won its independence from Mexico the year before, and in 1839 President Mirabeau B. Lamar appointed a commission to select a permanent site for the capital. Waterloo was chosen for its natural scenic beauty and central location, and the city was renamed in honor of one of the pioneer American settlers of Texas, Stephen F. Austin.

In 1845, Texas was annexed by the United States as the twenty-eighth state of the Union, and by 1860 the population had swelled up to 3,546. A large portion of the newcomers were of German descent and, along with their wagons and livestock, brought musical traditions in the form of choral singing and string ensembles.

One such German immigrant was a man named August Scholz, who in 1866 opened Scholz's Hall on the corner of Linden Street (now Seventeenth Street) and San Jacinto Boulevard. The hall and its adjoining "Biergarten" became a popular venue for German folk music and ensemble performances of all kinds. Remarkably, Scholz Garten has remained a popular venue for live music right on up to the present day. The barroom and music hall remain the oldest continuously operating business in the city of Austin.

In 1878, Austin contractor and businessman Captain Charles F. Millet built the Millet Opera House, which also remains standing on Ninth Street between Congress Avenue and Brazos Street. The three-story limestone

Saengerrunde picnic, June 1, 1894. *PICA 04907, Austin History Center, Austin Public Library.*

Scholz Garten, 1607, San Jacinto Boulevard. For nearly 150 years, this German-style "Biergarten" has provided Austinites with warm food, cold beer and ever-evolving forms of live music. *Photo courtesy of Larry D. Moore.*

Millett Opera House, 110 East Ninth Street. One of Texas's largest performance venues in the late nineteenth century, the building now houses a prominent social club. *Photo courtesy of Daniel R. Tobias.*

structure hosted opera, theater and other various events until its purchase by the Austin Independent School District in 1940.

One of the early chroniclers of Austin's musical legacy was longtime musician and concert organizer Mint O. James-Reed. The wife of music store owner John R. Reed, Mint wrote a book published in 1957 titled *Music in Austin, 1900–1956* that traces the local history of classical music performance.

Events such as the opening of the North Wing Auditorium in the University of Texas's Old Main Building in 1899 come back to life, as well as grand openings for the Majestic (later renamed Paramount) Theater in 1915 and UT's Hogg Memorial Auditorium in 1933. Reed also shares stories about some of Austin's earliest local musicians, including soprano Marguerite Huddle Slaughter, who moved to New York City to pursue a professional singing career before moving back to her hometown in 1933 to open a studio for "voice culture." Another prominent Austin musician from this period was pianist and music instructor Edmund Ludwig, who took countless aspiring local musicians under his wing and whom James-Reed describes as "possibly the greatest musician who ever lived in Austin."

As all of this was taking place, America's fascination with the frontier cowboy had come into full swing. Since the late 1800s, young men from throughout the Midwest and beyond had been moving down to Texas to take up a life of herding cattle across often harsh, sometimes hostile terrains. Some of these men took to playing guitar as a way of staving off the loneliness of the open range, and the age of the singing cowboy was born.

Songs such as "Git Along Little Dogies," "Sam Bass" and "Home on the Range" became popular folk tunes, representing a way of life in the American West. These songs would later inspire a University of Texas faculty member named John Lomax to collect and publish an anthology of the cowboy songs he remembered from his youth. In 1910, Lomax published *Cowboy Songs and Other Frontier Ballads*, a collection of folk lyrics that sparked national interest in folk music and brought Lomax nationwide fame.

Other early twentieth-century Austin musical pioneers included UT pre-law student and aspiring singer Woodward Maurice Ritter, whose interest in cowboy culture was fostered by faculty members such as Lomax and J. Frank Dobie.[1] In 1928, Ritter took a weekly gig as a singing cowboy on KPRC radio in Houston, and by the end of the year he had moved up to New York City and landed a role on Broadway. It was here that he earned the nickname "Tex," for which he would soon become world famous. In 1933, Tex Ritter made his first recordings for the American Record Corporation, and in 1936 he starred in the western film *Song of the Gringo*. Thus began a career in music and film that spanned over four decades and resulted in both a star on the Hollywood Walk of Fame in Los Angeles and an induction into the Country Music Hall of Fame in Nashville.[2]

Meanwhile, stars like Jimmie Rodgers (who briefly owned a home in the central Texas town of Kerrville), Ernest Tubb, Bob Wills and Hank Williams popularized the genre of country and western music and gave rise to the honky-tonk, which proliferated throughout Texas and the Southwest throughout the 1930s, '40s, '50s and '60s.[3]

In the 1940s and '50s, the American folk music revival swept from New York City across the United States, spurred by political and cultural dissent, which in turn led to a renewed interest in the work of artists such as Pete Seeger and Woodie Guthrie, as well as folklorists such as John Lomax and his son Alan. Once again, the University of Texas played a key role in the acculturation of the Capitol City; though much of Texas remained unaffected by social trends in other parts of the country, Austin was able to draw many different young, freethinking people from all walks of life from around the world.

Original Bob Wills tour bus outside the Broken Spoke at 3201 South Lamar Boulevard. From the 1930s to the mid-1950s, the "King of Western Swing" and his band, the Texas Playboys, were among the most popular acts in the country. *Photo courtesy of Opal Divine.*

Many of these Austin folkies and beatniks ended up hanging out at a small filling station turned beer joint on the outskirts of town. Kenneth Threadgill's filling station may have started out as a blue-collar bar, but it became forever linked with Austin's folk music scene and counterculture when he began hosting his Wednesday night hootenannies in the early 1960s. Threadgill was an easygoing man who accepted people of all walks of life despite his advanced age. This allowed him to befriend a group of folk revivalist UT students that included a decidedly countercultural young blues singer named Janis Joplin.

Joplin ran with a nonconformist group of proto-hippies that included future successful artists and musicians such as Gilbert Shelton, Jack Jackson and Powell St. John. The group's center of activity was a dilapidated former World War II army barracks across Nueces Street from Dirty Martin's hamburger stand. The old wooden house was known around UT campus simply as "the Ghetto."

Here, the fluctuating group of outcasts stayed up late, played music, dabbled in recreational drugs and tried to stay away from the law. Many of the individuals who came in and out of the Ghetto went on to various levels of success in the arts; because of this, the group has come to be recognized for helping to plant the seeds of Austin's reputation as a laid-back, hippie-friendly town.[4]

On November 22, 1963, President John F. Kennedy was assassinated in Dallas while on a presidential visit to Texas. He had been scheduled to appear in Austin later that day.

As with the rest of the country, the citizens of Austin were left speechless. Beyond the capitalized front-page headlines of the next day's *Austin American-Statesman*, page seven described the local scene:

> ### DISBELIEF, HORROR SHROUD CAPITAL CITY
> *There was very little activity on Congress Avenue Friday afternoon, where thousands of persons had been expected to witness the motorcade arrival of President John F. Kennedy.*
>
> *The Austin man-on-the-street expressed the seemingly universal reaction to news that the President had been assassinated—stunned disbelief and horror.*
>
> *The silver decorations put up on Congress early to add a festive note to Kennedy's arrival glittered brightly as men, women and teenagers snapped up copies of* The Austin Statesman[5] *to read of the tragedy.*
>
> *Mayor Lester Palmer and the City Council, who had proclaimed Friday as President John F. Kennedy Day in Austin, shut City Hall at 3p.m. in memorial to the President.*
>
> *The sudden story of the President's death was on the lips of young and old alike. Young men carrying transistor radios attracted knots of people to listen to news bulletins.*

Vice President Lyndon Baines Johnson, a Central Texas native and longtime political representative in both the U.S. House and Senate, was sworn in as thirty-sixth president of the United States on Air Force One at Dallas Love Field two hours after the assassination. A still-stricken nation reelected Johnson less than a year later based on his support of the civil rights movement and his apparent approval of de-escalation of U.S. involvement in the Vietnam War.[6]

As the nation continued to heal, Austin had matured into a steadily growing capital city of 214,000 by 1965. Known primarily for the University of Texas and for being the epicenter of Texas politics, the college town was also home to a handful of live music venues.

Beer joints such as Threadgill's, the 11th Door, the Skylark Club and the newly opened Broken Spoke Dancehall featured folk and country

The New Orleans Club, Eleventh Street and Red River, 1971. *PICH 06321, Austin History Center, Austin Public Library. Photo by Carl Hornberger.*

music, while the Jade Room, Club Saracen and the New Orleans Club hosted more rock-oriented acts. Meanwhile, venues such as the IL Club hosted popular R&B acts of the day, catering to Austin's heavily segregated East Side community. Similarly, southeast Austin venues such as Marie's Tearoom No. 2 and Bennies Club, as well as Sixth Street venues such as the Chaparral, La Plaza and the Green Spot, provided entertainment to Austin's large Hispanic population. Though ethnic boundaries were much more prominent in this period of Austin's history, the eventual confluence of musical styles would prove to play a major role in shaping the music of the next half century.

"It was the right time for music," remembers Wali King, bandleader of the jazz-soul ensemble the Afro-Caravan. "Jazz was popular, folk music was popular and then the rock scene was beginning to really stretch itself out. So people's ears were open to a lot of different kinds of sounds. It was a good time."

Folk, country, jazz and top 40 rock-and-roll were the dominant styles of music being played in the venues and on local radio. In the late 1950s, a tiny record label called Domino Records had issued a handful of singles, but it was an extremely small operation run by a few shareholders, and the label collapsed only a few years later.

Elvis Presley had made an Austin tour stop in August 1955 at a large auditorium on Barton Springs Road known as the Austin Sportcenter.[7] As the popularity of rock-and-roll spread among the American youth, more and more bands formed in garages across the country. Longtime Austin musician and future Sonobeat recording artist John Inmon recalls the social factors that led to the rock-and-roll era:

> *A lot of* [early rock-and-roll music] *was driven by this massive generation that came to be known as the boomers. There never has been—and it doesn't look like there's one on the horizon—a birthrate like there was after World War II. And so everybody was coming of age at around that time, seeking their own identity and all that kind of stuff. You couldn't deny the numbers, it was overwhelming to society. And at that point in time there wasn't the diversity of communication that there is now. There were three* [television] *networks, and each town had a few radio stations, and that's it. Everybody got their information from the same place, and it was easy for the generation to cohere. And it was unstoppable. Everything that we went for as a generation just sort of came into being by force of numbers.*

When the Beatles hit American airwaves in the early months of 1964, another guitar craze ensued. The best local rock-and-roll bands honed their skills playing top 40 covers at fraternity parties, as well as the occasional club gig. Though Austin had its fair share of musicians and venues, it was not yet particularly recognized as a "music town."

Local bands such as the Sweetarts, the Wig and the Babycakes would play the local rock circuit, which at the time involved mostly fraternity parties as opposed to bar gigs. "What a lot of people don't realize is that the UT fraternity party circuit had a huge impact on the formation of the Austin music scene," recalls Layton DePenning, guitarist, singer and songwriter for the Babycakes during this time period. "You could play two or three parties over the weekend as well as a club gig, and all the musicians would make enough money to pay the rent."

Fraternity party gigs required bands to play three- or four-hour-long sets populated by the biggest hits of the day, along with the occasional original composition snuck in between covers. "We'd pick up the newest single by

The Band or James Brown on a Tuesday," recalls Ernie Gammage. "By Friday night we'd have it down and play it in our sets."

As the counterculture movement gained more and more momentum throughout the 1960s, the fraternity party circuit became increasingly less popular. However, in the early days of rock music, the party scene was a primary source of income for local bands looking for their big break.

On September 24, 1965, Bob Dylan made a tour stop at Austin's Municipal Auditorium on Riverside Drive just south of Town Lake. His landmark album *Highway 61 Revisited* had been released the month before, and his hit song "Like a Rolling Stone" was the hottest thing in rock-and-roll. It was his first live appearance with his new backing band, Levon and the Hawks, which later came to be known simply as The Band.

The show was a huge hit with the four-thousand-strong Austin crowd and quite possibly inspired a whole new wave of singer/songwriters and rock-and-rollers right there on the spot.

One of the audience members of that show was an intellectually gifted and philosophically inclined UT student from Memphis named Tommy Hall. Dylan's show that night had a profound impact on Hall, who would soon join up with Roky Erickson, Stacy Southerland, John Ike Walton and Benny Thurmon to form the 13th Floor Elevators, innovators of psychedelic rock and one of the most iconic bands in the history of Austin music.

The Elevators quickly stood out among Austin bands for their obvious talent and for their unique sound, straddling the line between upbeat party rock-and-roll band and underground counterculture experimentalists. Lead singer Roky Erickson howled wild, primal screams between verses, while Tommy Hall played an otherworldly electric jug and Stacy Southerland ripped out hard-edged garage rock guitar riffs over Walton and Thurmon's rock-solid rhythm section.

The group fused an incendiary mixture of Stones-influenced rhythm and blues with an LSD-soaked counterculture ethos that instantly attracted a wide fan base among the Austin subculture, as well as notoriety among the Austin establishment.

> *Ernie Gammage: One late summer the Sweetarts were playing a week's worth of frat gigs in New Orleans. I recall hearing "You're Gonna Miss Me" over the speakers in a sandwich shop and thinking, "Shit! That's the big time!"*

> *Layton DePenning: The first time I saw the 13th Floor Elevators was in late 1965. I was a green kid just out of east Texas. I knew nothing*

about psychedelic music or psychotropic drugs at that time. I just stood in the middle of the Jade Room dance floor like a fool and let the cosmic waves of pure energy pour over me. They certainly had something special that emanated from the band. It was as powerful as it was indescribable. Psychedelic rock!

A 13th Floor Elevators promotional poster for a show at the Vulcan Gas Company, late 1960s. *Poster design by Gilbert Shelton.*

The Elevators gained a steady following by playing rock clubs such as the Jade Room and the New Orleans Club, two popular nightclubs just north of downtown. Eventually, the attendance at their shows began to number in the high hundreds, and an independent record label in Houston called International Artist signed them to its roster.

The deal proved to be a financial disaster for the band. IA was being run by a group of lawyers who had little interest in the music itself but sought to capitalize on the success of rock-and-roll bands such as the Beatles and the Rolling Stones. Nonetheless, the group did manage to release a hit single titled "You're Gonna Miss Me" that climbed to number fifty-five in the Billboard Charts, as well as two highly acclaimed full-length albums. The band moved to San Francisco for a short stint and then moved back to Texas, but eventually the combination of inner-band quarreling, shady business practices by their label and management, constant run-ins with the local police and virtually nonstop abuse of drugs and alcohol led to the band's eventual breakup.[8]

In 1967, a five-piece, southern-psychedelic rock band from San Antonio moved to Austin and also signed with International Artists. Bubble Puppy—their name derived from a fictitious children's game in Aldous Huxley's *Brave New World*—struck top 40 gold with their 1969 hit "Hot Smoke & Sassafras." As with the Elevators, the success of the single led to the prompt release of the band's debut album, titled *A Gathering of Promises*. And also as with the Elevators, the band became embroiled in conflicts with International Artists, inducing them to part ways with the label in 1970, after which they relocated to Los Angeles.

As the '60s counterculture movement continued to spread, the more experimental psychedelic bands would play at a new venue called the Vulcan Gas Company. Opened in the fall of 1967 on the southwest corner of Congress and Fourth Streets, the Vulcan quickly became a safe haven for longhaired artists and musicians influenced by bands such as the Beatles, Cream, Jefferson Airplane and the Doors. Ed Guinn, bassist for the popular local rock band the Conqueroo, remembers the impact the club's opening had on Austin's youth culture:

> *Austin was the kind of town where there was maybe, you'd see no more than fifty or sixty people that you'd want to be around. I mean literally. Everybody else was pretty straight, pretty square. And so there was that kind of core group of people that I'd known for by that point four or five years, and then the newer folks were coming into town, the students who*

were brave enough to come in. Because it was "off limits," you know, to students as it were. But it was just a big party, pretty exciting as I remember. Because we'd never seen anything like it, never done anything like it. The standard model in those days was a little, you know, kind of grimy cinder block rectangle called a club and you'd go in there and grind out something that you hoped was appealing to gather a crowd. This felt a lot bigger, felt a lot more forward thinking. Less of the past and more of the future. It was an interesting time, kind of an open audience, people that were open to new stuff and interesting ways of doing stuff, and we were lucky to have that audience and exposure. And the Gas Company was a smart, clever idea that spawned things like the Armadillo and other efforts around the country. They realized that you could do fresh, creative stuff and find an audience for it, you could get bands that were pretty outside of the mainstream and get people in front of them. And some of them connected.

The Vulcan, for much of its existence, also served as both home and art studio to Austin artist Jim Franklin.[9] Through the years, Franklin, along with fellow artists such as Guy Juke and Michael Priest, contributed as much to Austin's growing cultural scene as the town's many highly touted musicians did. Franklin recalls:

I lived in the building of the Vulcan. That was my studio, I slept there. Living there was an interesting experience…During the week, of course, it was a nice big building, and I had the whole top floor. Also, when we expanded to the corner of the next building over, there was a space there between HR Block and us. There was a storefront there, and it went back and joined an office kind of structure that went all the way to Fourth Street. And we got that space too, and then we cut an opening in the wall of the dance floor and used that other room as the concession stand. My room was in the office section, and the door opened on Fourth Street. It had a tall ceiling, taller than 12 feet, and there was a mezzanine in the office with a little rail around it and stairs leading down to the main room. And I could keep track of what was going on down there just by walking to the edge of the mezzanine. So kind of an interesting space. Downtown Austin was kind of depressed. The only things that were downtown were businesses, administrative buildings and some shops on Congress Avenue. And Sixth Street would have been sort of the weekend street; that was sort of the mall. Congress Avenue had the sort of high-dollar shops, and Sixth Street had the bars and the cheap shops. And it always was established that way, so

Number 316 Congress Avenue. From 1967 to 1970, this building housed the Vulcan Gas Company. Today, it is occupied by the Patagonia clothing chain. *Author's collection.*

people would come to town, this was the shopping mall. There were no other malls. And you wouldn't go to a small town, you'd go to the biggest town around. That's the way it all worked. That all got shifted, of course, when everything got supercharged with automobiles and urban sprawl. But that was that period when an artist, you wouldn't go out and find a barn to use as a studio, you'd go downtown and find an abandoned warehouse. Try to befriend the owners and see if they would rent it. And a lot of times they would. I mean there were no requirements, you know?

Rents were cheap, the atmosphere was relatively laid-back and there were plenty of gigs to be had in LBJ-era Austin. The civil rights movement and the escalating conflict in Vietnam were changing the way younger people looked at the world. In the midst of all this, the city of Austin would soon undergo a transformation of its own.

Cactus Pryor (front) and Packer Jack Wallace on-air at KTBC, circa 1960s. *PICA 05760, Austin History Center, Austin Public Library.*

Austin Radio and KAZZ-FM

B y the mid-1960s, local radio had blossomed since its initial proliferation forty years earlier. In Austin, AM radio station 1490 KNOW was the most popular in town, blasting out the latest top 40 rock and R&B hits to car radios and stereo systems throughout central Texas.

Station 1300 KVET-AM featured ABC network news delivered by Paul Harvey and Edward P. Morgan, as well as coverage of Astros baseball games. Station 590 KTBC provided CBS network news alongside local news, weather reports and special features, and 1370 KOKE played country-western music.

On the FM dial, 98.3 KHFI played classical music, utilizing the higher-fidelity (but shorter-reaching) FM signal. Station 90.7 KUT-FM provided the "voice of the University of Texas," broadcasting a combination of music programming and public affairs from noon to midnight.

Meanwhile, fledgling FM station 95.5 KAZZ broadcast a mix of pop, classical, folk, country and jazz music from a tiny 250-watt transmitter on the tenth floor of the Perry-Brooks Building in Downtown Austin. KAZZ, an unassuming small-frequency station that operated out of a modest four-room suite, would prove to have a profound impact on both Austin music and the entire radio industry in the coming years.

In their expansive and informative website chronicling the history of Sonobeat Records, brothers Bill Josey Jr. and Jack Josey provide a detailed and comprehensive narrative of both the record label and KAZZ. Through the website, which was used as a primary source for this book, as well as

The extensively remodeled Perry-Brooks Building at 720 Brazos Street. KAZZ-FM broadcast out of the tenth floor in the mid- to late 1960s. *Photo from author's collection.*

through my conversations with Bill, who now works as a business and legal executive for Discovery Communications in Los Angeles, I became aware of how the story of KAZZ is central to the story of Sonobeat Records. From this tiny little FM radio station transmitting out of downtown Austin, the inspiration for Sonobeat Records would eventually take root. Both Sonobeat and KAZZ played a highly important role in the development of the Austin music scene.

In the early days of radio, almost all broadcasts were conducted on the far-reaching AM signal. It wasn't until the late 1950s that the higher-fidelity FM band began to catch on as an alternative. Though FM broadcasts cannot produce as wide a coverage area as the AM band, they are much less vulnerable to electrical interference and produce a clearer sound.

On March 23, 1956, Austin's first FM station, KHFI, made its initial broadcast, playing classical music on the clearer signal. The station had been subsidized by James E. Moore, who owned a hi-fidelity audio equipment store and was hoping to boost sales. An avid jazz fan, Moore founded KAZZ the following year as Austin's first FM jazz station, broadcasting out of the same building that housed his retail business.

Eight years later, local restaurateur Monroe Lopez purchased KAZZ and relocated it to the Perry-Brooks Building on the corner of Seventh Street and Brazos. Along with the change of location, Lopez expanded the programming to include popular music, show tunes, light classical music and Spanish pop hits.

In September 1964, Bill Josey Jr., then entering his freshman year at UT, was hired as an afternoon disc jockey, adopting the radio moniker "Rim Kelley." Bill had grown up in Austin, attending William B. Travis High School, and his father, Bill Sr., commuted to Galveston each week to work as sales manager for top 40 AM station KILE.

Encouraged by his father, Rim[10] was able to convince KAZZ station manager Gib Divine to let him play rock-and-roll music during his four o'clock timeslot. Though it is hard to imagine today, rock-and-roll was almost exclusively limited to AM radio at the time. The farther-reaching AM frequency meant more listeners, and few programmers considered that their audience would care too much about the fidelity of rock-and-roll music. Rim urged Divine to give it a try.

The experiment proved to be a success with KAZZ listenership and even made national news. On June 21, 1965, *Billboard Magazine* ran a profile by weekly columnist Claude Hall titled "KAZZ Specializes in Not Specializing."

"Top 40 music on an FM station?" began the article. "Yes sir, along with folk and country music. The station is KAZZ-FM and the programming is 'many types of music to suit many tastes.'"

The article tells the story of Rim Kelley and KAZZ's subtle yet unprecedented innovation in radio programming, describing KAZZ as the only FM station in central Texas that "has the guts" to incorporate

KAZZ-FM Starline
Record survey.
*Courtesy of the Sonobeat
Historical Archives.*

top 40 rock-and-roll in its formatting. The article also underscores an important aspect of KAZZ that would later have a significant influence on the formation of the Austin music scene: the station was extremely eclectic for its time.

"The station is the only Central Texas outlet for folk music; the prime source of jazz in Central Texas, and the area outlet for WSM's Grand Ole

Opry show," the article points out. This eclecticism proved to be a success with listeners, attracting a younger, more diverse crowd and resulting in an expansion of Rim Kelley's time slot by two additional hours.

Around this time, Bill Josey Sr. was hired by KAZZ as full-time sales manager. A lifelong fan of both music and technology, Bill Sr. was born in Houston in 1921 and attended the University of Texas, eventually earning a master's degree in psychology. After serving as a naval officer in World War II, Josey moved back to Houston and opened a psychology practice. The years shortly after the war were prosperous ones; it was the dawn of the Cold War era, and many companies in the chemical and oil-producing industries had high demand for psychologists who could detect whether employees were secretly communists. Bill Josey Jr. recalls:

> *I think that generally you could call the Red Scare an epic period in American history. If you had any talent at isolating or identifying communists, then you had a job with the government or for the government or with companies that had government contracts. As an industrial psychologist, you administered personality tests, IQ tests…the kinds of tests that industry would use to identify people who were best suitable or not suitable for particular jobs that they were considering hiring them for.*

The elder Josey's line of work had him traveling throughout the region, administering personality tests for government-related companies throughout the east Texas portion of the Gulf Coast. After roughly a decade of prosperity, widespread paranoia of communism began to wane, and so too did the demand for psychologists who were able to identify them. Unable to find substantial work as a psychologist, and now with a wife and four children to care for, Bill and his family relocated back to Austin the following year. Applying his psychology background to sales, Bill eventually landed the job in Galveston radio that would ultimately lead him to KAZZ in 1965.

Bill fit right in to the nascent Austin music scene. Though in his late forties, he remained receptive to the music being made by the younger generation. He was an early supporter of the 13th Floor Elevators; when top 40 station KNOW refused to play the band's music on air, Bill continued to push the band heavily on KAZZ. Roky Erickson had been a high school friend of Rim, and when Roky was indicted on drug charges in 1966, Bill even testified as a character witness on his behalf:

After the Elevators were busted for marijuana—and keep in mind, this was the early days of marijuana—it was difficult for them to get jobs then, because the fear was that they would smoke pot on stage. The law would come in and it could be a bad scene, bad public relations for the local clubs who have to depend upon people coming to their place to dance and have fun in order to continue as a club. So at that time [marijuana] was really pretty bad. If you put it on a scale of 1 to 10, it was a value of 10. It was pretty rough. So I went to the grand jury on their behalf. I was not for the marijuana user, because I figured that if their music doesn't turn them on, and they needed a crutch to turn them on, then they weren't really much of a musician in my eyes. I felt like their music, what they were actually doing should turn them on. I know that a lot of performers have to have something to loosen up…like in the case of Janis Joplin, she needed Southern Comfort. As long as I can remember, she had to have her fifth of Southern Comfort right there on the floor. And she picked it up like someone would a Coke or something, and she took swigs of it as if it were a Coke! And before long that whole fifth of Southern Comfort was gone. And other musicians have to have some kind of alcoholic beverage to relieve the tension, I suppose. Alright, to relieve the tension was then the key word. So why'd they use marijuana? I figured it was to relieve tension. So I went to…our radio station was in the Perry-Brooks Building, and downstairs was Ed Meyer, a pharmacist. So I ask him about it, and he broke out his pharmacopoeia. And we looked in there about marijuana, and I said, "I've got to have this Xeroxed." So I took that Xeroxed page out of the pharmacopoeia to the grand jury, and I just proceeded to read it right out of there. That "marijuana at one time was prescribed by physicians for migraine headaches because it was a depressant." And I said, "Okay, now these fellows smoked marijuana, which neither you nor I agree should be done, because it's illegal, but I just want to point out that it's not going to make them violent. They're not gonna jump up and kill somebody or do something of violence. If anything, it's going to make them tired, sleepy, or less tense." And so that went over pretty good, you know, that made a little sense.

Shortly after joining KAZZ, Bill Sr. attained the title of general and commercial manager. Around this time, the station began to feature remote broadcasts of live music performances around Austin every Wednesday, Friday, Saturday and Sunday evening. These started with live broadcasts of jazz bands at the Club Seville and subsequently grew to include rock shows at the Jade Room and Club Saracen, as well as folk sets by up-and-coming artists such as Jerry Jeff Walker, Townes Van Zandt and Janis Joplin at the 11th Door. Josey remembers:

> *Back in those days you didn't even get releases from these people. You just showed up, the owner of the club paid for you to come in and do the live remote because it promoted them, it was like an hour-long ad to get people to come down. It was even before people did seven-second delays. The most interesting thing that I remember happening during any of these broadcasts was Janis Joplin broke out into a series of profanities in between songs, reached down to get her Jack Daniels bottle or whatever she was drinking that night and we'd have to quickly turn down the microphone in front of her and send it back to the studio for a commercial while my dad would go try to calm her down and tell her that you can't say these things on live radio. But she was out of control, I think we did a couple of broadcasts with her and we gave up. She was incorrigible—her language was incorrigible! She was a great talent, but she didn't work on live radio.*

In an interview with Doug Hanners in August 1976, Bill Sr. credits Dallas-based CBS Records sales executive Joe Mansfield for suggesting he go into the recording business:

> *He used to go with us on remote broadcasts just to have a little fun out of it. And we would broadcast live from the club every night. There were an awful lot of groups that we used to broadcast that way. 13th Floor Elevators, Janis Joplin, [Townes] Van Zandt, Jerry Jeff Walker, Mance Lipscomb. [We broadcast from the] 11th Door, also from the New Orleans Club. They had a good variety of entertainment. And Joe said that I really ought to get into recording, because there was so much talent in town.*

Conducting the remote broadcasts put Bill and Rim in a unique position to monitor the pulse of the bourgeoning Austin music scene while simultaneously exposing them to the equipment and craft of audio engineering. Working at the radio station was naturally beneficial in this regard as well, as many local groups would bring their demos to the station in hopes of gaining local exposure.

Having shared lifelong interests in music and technology, it seemed only natural that the two men would venture into the recording business. By the latter half of 1966, Bill and Rim were in the planning stages of launching an independent record label. They had the equipment and the resources in the form of KAZZ's Ampex 354 professional two-track tape recorder, and they commissioned KAZZ chief engineer Bill Curtis to design and build a portable stereo mixer. They had all the pieces; now they just needed to figure out how to bring them all together.

Up to this point, Austin's musical history was not particularly unique. Aside from the anomaly of an FM station that played top 40 rock-and-roll music (which would later become an industry standard), there was little to distinguish Austin's musical landscape from that of any other mid-sized college town.

New York City had been the United States' most important cultural center since the early nineteenth century, and the success of Midtown's Broadway theater district led to the foundation of numerous sheet music publishing companies based around the area known as Tin Pan Alley. This small section of Midtown Manhattan produced some of the earliest and longest-lasting standards in American popular music, and when the gramophone and radio industries took off in the early twentieth century, New York remained an important musical center.

In 1965, New York was still one of the most populous cities in the world, an undisputed cultural mega-capital that was home to the nation's largest record labels, publishers, radio shows and broadcast market. The immense music and entertainment industry that grew out of New York City represents a big-city model for the formation of a music scene, with emphasis on establishing markets and maximizing profits. Other major commercial music centers such as London and Chicago developed in similar fashion.

On the West Coast, Los Angeles's music scene had developed when it was still a relatively small city in the 1930s and '40s. Though it lacked the sheet music publishing industry that was central to New York's musical development, the city was home to a vibrant African American community that congregated around Central Avenue and produced such talents as Charles Mingus, Buddy Collette and Gerald Wilson.

In 1942, Capitol Records was established and would soon become one of the largest and most important labels in the United States. Its iconic headquarters building at 1750 Vine Street, completed in 1956, ensured that Los Angeles would remain a major musical center for decades to come.

In the late 1960s, a handful of highly influential bands broke through to national prominence out of the numerous music venues that dotted the Sunset Strip; such bands included the Byrds, Buffalo Springfield and The

Doors. These bands, though short-lived, represented the first wave of post-Beatle rock-and-roll bands that moved to Los Angeles in order to hit the big time. The trend has continued up to the present day.

To the north, the San Francisco sound had developed out of the vast counterculture community centered on Haight-Ashbury. Its drug-fueled psychedelic scene was already starting to attract young nonconformists from across the country, including Austin transplant and future rock star Janis Joplin. Detroit already had a rich history as a center for blues, gospel and jazz music, and in 1959, Barry Gordy Jr. founded Motown Records, which would go on to produce a seemingly endless string of number one hits and become synonymous with soul and R&B music. Chicago and New Orleans had been famous centers for jazz and blues since the turn of the century, and Memphis was still one of the hottest label hubs on the planet with the continuing success of Sun and Stax Records. In Nashville, the nationally syndicated *Grand Ole Opry* radio show had made the Ryman Auditorium its permanent home in 1943, solidifying Nashville's importance as America's "country music capital."

Austin was nowhere near these cities in terms of industry, but one thing it did have was a large talent pool of Texas musicians. Tommy Taylor, an accomplished drummer and vocalist who has played with Eric Johnson, Christopher Cross, Eliza Gilkyson and Double Trouble, grew up in Austin during the late 1960s and remembers the perceived difference between his hometown and other industry cities:

> Austin was a small town; those places were entertainment centers. They had an infrastructure, and an entertainment infrastructure. New York, obviously being the first major city in the United States, all of the industry was there. When they got tired of the snow and the unions and the hassle, they moved to California and then all of the unions followed. And it's cool, too, because I like the protection for the workers and the artist. I mean, in this industry, for the side men and other things, you really need a little bit of help, or people will just take advantage of you. And they do here in Austin still, there's still no infrastructure here! I mean, that's the problem. Nashville was the same thing: the country music scene was there, and they had the industry, they had the recording studios, they had the managers, they had the hits being made from there and everything. But the one great thing about the [Austin] music scene, when I was a kid, the older guys like Ernie [Gammage] and Pat Whitefield and Rusty [Wier] and John Inmon and Vince Mariani

40

and that whole group of people, they were so supportive. They took me under their wing. It wasn't like, "Let's see what we can do to keep this kid down"; it was like, "Let's see what we can do to give this kid a launching pad." But it was a launching pad to nowhere!

Sonobeat Records would soon establish itself as an early outlet in a town where few opportunities beyond a frat party or club gig existed. By recording Austin's local talent, it gave voice to the emerging scene and offered a glimpse of what the city would soon become.

University of Texas campus, circa 1965. *PICA 14557, Austin History Center, Austin Public Library.*

A Picture of Me

The Formation of Sonobeat Records

Three years after the assassination of President Kennedy, unthinkable tragedy again struck in the state of Texas. This time Austin itself was the setting for nation-rattling headlines. On the first day of August 1966, UT engineering student and former U.S. Marine sharpshooter Charles Whitman murdered his mother and then his wife before transporting a small arsenal to the University of Texas Tower. After killing three more civilians inside the tower, he barricaded himself in and proceeded to shoot forty-one people from the twenty-eighth-floor observation deck.

The siege lasted ninety-six terrifying minutes before law enforcement was able to make its way up the tower and kill the sniper. The massacre made national headlines, including the covers of *Time* and *Life* magazines, and directly led to the formation of SWAT (Special Weapons and Tactics) teams across the country. No one ever imagined anything like it would ever occur in the laid-back central Texas college town. Tommy Taylor remembers:

I was listening to KAZZ on my front porch when Whitman started shooting. And if memory serves me, either very shortly before that or during that time period the song of the summer was "Summer in the City" by the Lovin' Spoonful. And I can remember that. I mean, I can picture myself...Austin is hot in August, and we had a polished concrete front porch with the roof overhung. And I could run the extension cord out, and you got better reception outside with the FM. So I'd lay on the cool, polished concrete porch with my shirt off and my cut-offs while listening to KAZZ in the afternoon. And I was literally listening to KAZZ when my neighbor came over and said—'cause my sister went to UT—he said, "There's a crazy man on the tower shooting people with a rifle. Is your sister okay?" I said, "Yeah, she's at work." She worked at Sears in the record department. But KAZZ was on the radio and I remember them coming on and going, "We've cut to UT," and whatever they said. It was like, "Wow." And you've got to realize, Austin, Texas, was like Mayberry, man. I mean, this kind of stuff didn't go on here.

Eventually, life returned to normal on the tragedy-stricken University of Texas campus and in the city of Austin. The music continued to play on KNOW and KAZZ and in the local venues around town.

Meanwhile, Bill Josey and Rim Kelley continued to formulate the blueprint for their as-yet-unnamed recording enterprise. They had the resources along with a vast knowledge of the Austin music scene; now they simply needed to test their skills as producers of recorded sound.

The first band they chose to work with was the local rock outfit Leo and the Prophets. A five-piece garage rock band, the group had risen to local prominence as the house band for the Ozone Forest nightclub.

The session was held in the spring of 1967 in the parking lot of the Lake Austin Inn. The results yielded three songs; however, Bill and Rim lacked sufficient engineering experience, and the recordings were deemed un-releasable. Bill Josey Jr. recalls:

We didn't have a recording studio, so we went to the same clubs where we had broadcast from. And we would rent their ballroom or their facility, usually earlier in the afternoon or on a day when they would otherwise be closed. We'd take the equipment in, and my dad was in charge of scrounging up the bands and the facilities, and I was in charge of figuring out how to produce the sound. And from there we essentially built Sonobeat on the proverbial shoestring budget. We had a good friend named John Early, who was managing Leo and the Prophets. We couldn't afford to go buy a professional mixer, so I worked with the KAZZ engineer and he put together a transistorized six-channel mixer for us. And we needed to test it out, so John agreed that Leo and the Prophets would be a good test case for us. So we went out and recorded with them…The real test was not so much the music. They were a rock-and-roll band, they were pretty well known, so we knew it would be fun. But the recording was terrible. It was distorted…it just was terrible in every possible way. It was a disaster. So we had to go back to the drawing board and figure out what was wrong, why the microphones were distorting, what we would actually have to do to be able to record a microphone in front of a stack of speakers driven by a Marshal amp that was going to be blaring at full steam ahead. So ultimately our engineer figured out how to fix that, and then it was up to my dad and I to figure out how to get a good recording.

Though the sessions did not result in an official release, Leo and the Prophets would continue to have success in the local music scene, releasing the regionally successful single "Tilt-a-Whirl" backed with "Parking Meter" on Totem Records in April 1967.

For their next attempt, Bill and Rim recorded the Lee Arlano Trio, an all-acoustic instrumental jazz combo from Pueblo, Colorado, that regularly toured the Southwest jazz club circuit. Drummer and bandleader Lee Arlano, bassist Andy Arlano and pianist Sam Poni had been working the western U.S. jazz circuit for several years, touring out to the West Coast and down through Arizona and Texas. When they came through Austin, they played at the Club Seville, located at the Sheraton Crest Inn (now the Radisson Hotel) on the southeast corner of Congress Avenue and First Street (now Cesar Chavez).

Having established themselves as a popular touring jazz band, the Lee Arlano Trio had already done several live remote broadcasts on KAZZ. Bill and Rim had already been impressed by the group, and recognizing the logistical ease of recording an all-acoustic act, they decided the trio would make an ideal group to record for Sonobeat. The band agreed, and a session was scheduled, using the Club Seville itself as a makeshift recording facility.

Songs recorded during the session included the popular Harry Warren–Mack Gordon jazz standard "There Will Never Be Another You," as well as the Newton Mendonco–Antonio Carlos Jobim bossa nova tune "Meditation." Listening to the recordings today, they are remarkable for their increased clarity over the Leo and the Prophets recordings. The musicianship is tight, and the sound jumps off the grooves of the 45rpm record, transporting the listener back to the Austin, Texas, of the late 1960s.

Bill and Rim were happy with the quality of the recording and decided they would release a single. However, they also decided that they wanted their first release to feature a more marketable rock-and-roll band.

"We figured rock was gonna sell better," recalls Bill Josey Jr. "We decided we'd better establish our label's name with a rock single first; then we can try the jazz single."

Around this time, Rim's younger brother, Jack Josey, had started working as a DJ at KAZZ as well. Jack remembers:

I was fourteen when my father and brother started Sonobeat. Like my brother, I was a Top 40 DJ at KAZZ-FM. I had a Saturday show during the school year and a Monday through Saturday on-air shift in the summer. However, I didn't participate in Sonobeat other than to give my dad occasional critiques of various recordings he'd play for me. My most common suggestion was to raise the volume on the vocalist. Most of the Sonobeat recording sessions were either while I was in school or late at night when I was asleep.

Working in radio had introduced Bill and Rim to many of the up-and-coming musicians that composed the late 1960s Austin music scene. While Austin had not yet gained the reputation it would make for itself in the next decade, there were a handful of talented bands and musicians playing the fraternity party circuit, as well as the occasional club gig.

One such band was a four-piece R&B-inflected group called the Sweetarts. Consisting of guitarist/vocalist Ernie Gammage, bassist Pat Whitefield, vocalist Mike Galbraith, keyboardist Tom Van Zandt and drummer Dwight Dow, the band had made a name for itself as an up-tempo party band, bashing out the latest rock and R&B hits at frat parties and dances on the weekends.

The Sweetarts came together when Gammage, a UT student originally from Houston, left his first band, the Fabulous Chevelles, to start a new group in 1965. The band gelled quickly and immediately went to work, often playing three or four several-hour-long gigs each weekend. The sets started with covers of the top hits of the day—the Beatles, the Beau Brummels, Otis Redding, the Byrds—and every now and then the band would sneak an original or two into the set. Eventually, the Sweetarts built up a solid fan base and cut a seven-inch single for the Dallas-based Vandan label in the summer of 1966.

Bill and Rim had been aware of the group; a copy of the Vandan single had made its way into Rim's hands, and he had played it on his rock-and-roll show on KAZZ. This prompted Rim to book the band for the station's live broadcast series, held at Club Saracen on February 16, 1967. A recording of this broadcast still survives and begins with nighttime KAZZ deejay Kirk Wilson's introduction: "Our live remote broadcast comes from the Club Saracen at 1809 San Jacinto in Austin, Texas. The music of the Sweetarts, your host from dial 95 Rim Kelley. Rim, are you there?"

The Sweetarts, 1967. *Photo courtesy of Ernie Gammage.*

Rim responds:

> *Yes, thank you very much, Kirk. Tonight: happening sounds. The Sweetarts, who do indeed have a hit record, number 21 on the KAZZ Starline Survey, and on the other stations' survey, and...well, they're great. I can't say much more, except that we are live at the Club Saracen, 1809 San Jacinto Street in Austin tonight, and I've asked the Sweetarts to open up their set tonight with their very, very good song, "So Many Times." So here it goes, everybody.*

Impressed once again, Rim offered to record the Sweetarts for the new Sonobeat label.

The sessions with the Sweetarts began on July 18, 1967, at the Swingers Club in North Austin. The initial session yielded the basic instrumental tracks for two songs, followed by an overdub session several days later at the KAZZ studio in downtown Austin. Additional vocals, tambourine and shaker were added to the basic tracks, and the single was deemed ready for release.

Once completed, the recordings were sent to the lacquer-mastering engineer at Houston Records, where the physical copies were pressed. "A Picture of Me," backed with "Without You," was released as Sonobeat stereo single R-s101, and the Sonobeat record label was born.

Sonobeat single R-s101 "A Picture of Me." *Courtesy of Sonobeat Historical Archives.*

"A Picture of Me" captures the energy and excitement of a young band striving for a shot at the big time. It is a musical snapshot of the time period, featuring concisely syncopated bass and guitar lines rumbling beneath a psychedelic Farfisa organ, which subsequently gives way to choppy phrases of open chords and a stop-start drum dynamic. The vocal delivery, along with the performance of the rest of the band, is right on cue, and it is easy to see why Bill and Rim chose it as Sonobeat's first single. The B-side, "Without You," displays more of a country/blues garage rock slant, influenced by the early work of the Beatles and the Rolling Stones.

For the label's debut release, Bill and Rim employed a subtly innovative recording technique, which tied into their FM radio background. At the time, 45rpm records were generally issued in monaural sound, or

"A Picture of Me." *Courtesy of Sonobeat Historical Archives.*

"mono," meaning that the total recorded sound went through a single channel. In other words, if a record player had two speakers, the same exact sound would be heard from either one. Since 45rpm singles were designed for airplay on single-frequency AM radio, stereo pressings were considered unnecessary.[11]

Naturally drawn to the advancing technology of the time, Bill and Rim decided to release all Sonobeat singles in stereo, partly because of preference in sound quality and partly because it would help their small, homespun label stand out among potential record buyers. Additionally, the record was packaged in a custom picture sleeve featuring a publicity photo of the band, an eye-catching enhancement to the typical blank-sleeve single releases of the time period. This gave both band and label added visibility on the shelves of local record stores.

"A Picture of Me," as one would expect, received a healthy dosage of airplay on KAZZ and led the band to new opportunities around Austin. Having a single on the radio, albeit a small FM station, exposed the band to a wider audience and helped its draw at club gigs such as the Jade Room and the Saracen.

The single even garnered some national press when the weekly trade publication *Cashbox* magazine ran a review in its October 6 edition. The periodical described the single as "set out of the run-of-the-mill category by excellent stereo recording that should bring considerable attention among discerning teens and disco listeners."

Sonobeat's debut release gave one of the top party bands in Austin additional buzz and exposure. The Sweetarts continued to perform around town, and Bill and Rim continued to develop the Sonobeat brand. The label had been launched; now it was up to the father and son to expand the label's repertoire.

For the next Sonobeat single, they decided to release the previously recorded Lee Arlano Trio material. The jazz record demonstrated Sonobeat's (and Austin's) eclecticism early on. To this day, the music scene in Austin is known for its wide variety of musical styles, and this was a key element of the scene from its earliest stages.

"All of those venues and all of those clubs added a dimension to Austin that you didn't find in a lot of other towns or cities," recalls Bill Josey Jr. "And that was the diversity of the music that we were starting to hear in Austin. Ultimately, I'm not surprised when I look back on it that Austin became the live music capital of the world."

Like the Sweetarts' record before it, the single sold modestly around Austin but did not break through to national prominence. However, with two singles under its belt, Sonobeat Records had begun to establish itself around Austin. Later in 1967, Sonobeat issued its third single, a recording of Willie Nelson's "Night Life" by Club Seville manager and house bandleader Don Dean. Though a competent singer and performer, the single was mostly recorded as a favor to a family friend; Dean had no real aspirations to become a popular recording artist, but as manager and talent buyer of Club Seville, he was constantly suggesting new artists for Bill and Rim to record.

Sonobeat issued one more single in 1967, returning its focus to youth-oriented rock-and-roll. The Lavender Hill Express had quickly established itself, along with the Sweetarts, as one of Austin's most popular up-and-coming rock bands. The band had its roots in an earlier rock-and-roll group called the Babycakes, which featured future Lavender Hill Express members Layton DePenning and Leonard Arnold. Arnold remembers:

> *We played at the Jade room every Thursday, but mainly we were doing fraternity parties there at the university. When we got the Babycakes together, we started rehearsing...Pat Russell, the drummer, went to church over there right off the drag, right across from the big student union building and all that. And there was a little church over there that had kind of a basement that you could see in from the ground, but you had to scoot down to these ground-level windows, kind of a basement situation. And we'd go in there and rehearse, and I mean we'd start rehearsing, and before long there were university people crammed in the building and all the way around it listening to the band. We got real popular with the university right there just rehearsing. And one night we were rehearsing and this gal walked in, her name was Paula something, and she had a little agency there, and she says, "I book bands, would y'all want somebody to help you? Call me." We did, and she started booking us at all those fraternity parties. And we were playing two fraternity parties almost every week, every Friday and Saturday.*

The Lavender Hill Express formed in 1966, when the Babycakes and another prominent Austin band called the Wig decided to merge their groups into a new band. Arnold recalls:

> *The Lavender Hill Express was a combination of two bands. Rusty's band was the Wig, and Layton and I had the Babycakes, and we joined forces. We were all playing down at the Jade room on different nights, just got to be friends. Anyway, Rusty and I were real good buddies, so we got to talking. Moby Grape came out with their first record, and it had all these really cool rock-and-roll songs on there, but cool harmony, kinda country-type harmony. And we decided we wanted to start a band that could do that. He didn't have any singers in his band, and we did. And Layton is the singer of all times for me, he's got the prettiest voice and he sang harmony really well with everybody. So that was why we started that band, the Lavender Hill Express. Country-rock was right down the alley we wanted to go, so we masterminded that thing. Turned into a pretty cool little band.*

DePenning adds:

> *We kind of put those two bands together, and they were pretty prominent party bands, frat bands. We did mostly covers, current covers, like the Animals and Stones, all the stuff that was current. And we kind of combined those two bands, and they were very popular, this was way before the development of music in Austin. It's always been here…some of the people [Bill Josey] recorded had been functioning before I got [to Austin]. But anyway, at some point we took the Lavender Hill Express and we almost immediately started writing original music. We were very enamored with all the stuff that was going on in music, singer-songwriter kind of things and bands and everything, certainly a golden age. We started writing, and so we got with Bill Josey and started recording.*

The new group consisted of DePenning and Arnold on guitar, Johnny Shwertner on keyboard, Jess Yaryan on bass and Rusty Wier on drums and lead vocals. They had the advantage of a built-in following, as well as a prominent Thursday night residency at the Jade Room in downtown Austin, and they were able to convince KNOW disc jockey Mike Lucas to sign on as their manager.

The Lavender Hill Express, circa 1969—Layton DePenning, guitar/vocals. *Photo courtesy of Layton DePenning.*

Leonard Arnold, guitar. *Photo courtesy of Layton DePenning.*

Jess Yaryan, bass. *Photo courtesy of Layton DePenning.*

Rusty Wier, drums/vocals. *Photo courtesy of Layton DePenning.*

Arnold remembers:

Mike was a deejay at KNOW, and we were looking for another manager, and we ran into Mike. And Mike was great; Mike's the best I've ever been around as far as somebody who takes care of business. So we turned it over to Mike, and from that time on we were busy three days a week every week. And we did real well. We were making as much then as I can make now playing in bars. We played the Jade Room in 1968. We were playing the Jade Room making a hundred, a hundred and a quarter apiece as a five-piece band. And that's after Mike got his percentage and we paid somebody to take money at the door [laughs]. It was great! We were the hottest thing in town down there for a long time.

"We almost immediately started writing original music," says DePenning. "We were very enamored by all the stuff that was going on in music, singer/songwriter kind of things."

The band met Bill and Rim through its new manager, and shortly thereafter the two parties agreed to cut a single. "Visions," backed with "Trying to Live a Life," is another strong example of the musical undercurrents that preceded Austin's rise to prominence in the entertainment industry. The music is joyful and upbeat, with rich harmonies and an overdubbed string quartet underscoring a strong Beatles influence. According to Arnold:

> *Bill really did a lot for all of us who were there in Austin trying to record stuff. They had that radio station over on Eighth or Ninth, around the corner from J.R. Reed Music. The first time we recorded it was over there. I actually had my guitar amp out in the hall. We were doing the sessions on a two-track machine, so we only had two passes. We'd put all the basics on one track, then put the vocals and the overdubs on another track. And we had to do everything at the same time, pretty much.*

DePenning adds:

> *I remember the building downtown—it's still there—the old office building where their radio station was. I remember doing vocals in one of the hallways, 'cause Rim Kelley was going for ambiance. I think we did the string section that way, too—a quartet, actually. And we had a clavinet solo…you know, it was just right out of that time period.*

Released Christmas week 1967, the record sold through its initial pressing within a matter of months. As with the Sweetarts, the record gave the band a new outlet with which to promote itself and reach the ears of new listeners around central Texas.

On December 12, 1967, Sonobeat held a recording session at the newly opened Vulcan Gas Company. The band it recorded was the South Canadian Overflow, which featured future Austin music stars Donny Dolan on drums and John Inmon on lead guitar. Though the recordings were never released, they marked the beginning of an extended relationship between the label and Inmon, who would record with Sonobeat two years later in the band Plymouth Rock.

By providing an outlet for local bands like the Sweetarts, the Lavender Hill Express and the South Canadian Overflow to record and promote their music, Sonobeat Records was able to stoke the musicians' creative flames while fostering a sense of encouragement and confidence in being able to "make it" in the music industry.

John Inmon recalls:

There was a culture among the musicians in town, because there were just so many kids. So many. There were just a lot of us, and you could charge a dollar at the door at a club, and if you could get five hundred kids in there, you'd have five hundred dollars. And at the time you could get a steak dinner for under two dollars and you could rent a nice two-, three-bedroom house for a hundred dollars a month. The cost of living was extremely low, and there was all this work to be had if you were a good band. If you could play, you would draw the kids in. And everybody was eyeing the music; everybody was really enthusiastic about the music. It was what we did, we grew our hair and we'd listen to the music, and we banded together. So it was easy to make it, and a lot of musicians started moving to town because of that. There were all these beautiful girls at the University of Texas and stuff; it was just like a musician's paradise. And for a lot of that period of time there were some enterprising disc jockeys at the local AM station. This was before FM really took hold. And one guy named Mike Lucas in particular…there were a couple of booking agents that would scarf up the good bands. And Bill Josey, who worked at [KAZZ], he was a gear nut. He just loved recording, and he loved radio and everything that had a tube in it; he really liked it. And he was interested in recording in particular, in multi-track recording. He had this open field of all these musicians that were out there playing, and he was a smart guy, and he realized that there was a market; there were all these kids that were spending all this money out there. And there were bands out there actually starting to write songs, and so he would, you know, sign them to a little contract. And sometimes not even sign them to a contract, just, "Come on up to the [studio]." And the bands would go in there and record, and he would put it out as Sonobeat. And these disc jockeys that were booking these bands would play their records. And so that gave us a little mini-market here in Austin, and that really helped to crystallize the music scene here, even in the mid- to late '60s that was happening. People usually associate the beginning of the Austin music scene with the early '70s, but it actually started a bit earlier. And Bill Josey had everything to do with that—Bill Josey, Mike Lucas, all those guys.

Ultimately, neither the Sweetarts nor the Lavender Hill Express would end up breaking out to national success, but in the next decade, many of the musicians involved with the two bands would become key figures in the development of the Austin music scene.

In January 1968, Monroe Lopez sold KAZZ.[12] The sale of the station ended Bill and Rim's tenure in FM radio; however, both men were now able to devote more time and energy to the development of Sonobeat Records.

"I remember hoping that [Sonobeat Records] would be successful…especially after KAZZ sold," recalls Jack Josey. "We were living in a nice neighborhood in northeast Austin near Reagan High School when KAZZ sold. I didn't want us to have to move."

Rim Kelley, still studying radio television and film at the University of Texas, picked up a part-time job as a weekend deejay for the major AM station KNOW. Bill concentrated on the label, recording one session after another.

The year 1968 would prove to be Sonobeat's busiest, most profitable one. Bill sent off copies of the single releases to every regional radio station or publication they could find. In April 1968, the regional lifestyle magazine *Go Central Texas* ran an article titled "Austin Now Recording Center with Hits Ahead," referring to the Lee Arlano Trio single and the rising profile of Sonobeat Records. It was one of the first articles touting Austin's live music scene, a clear indication that Sonobeat was playing a major role in establishing Austin as a music town.

Over the course of 1968, Bill and Rim held dozens of recording sessions with a wide array of musical acts, some local to Austin and some just passing through town. In February, they held another session at the Vulcan Gas Company, this time with the local psychedelic rock mainstays Shiva's Headband.

Shiva's Headband had been formed some years earlier by fiddler Spencer Perkins and his wife, Susan. The band included keyboardist Shawn Siegel, guitarists Kenny Parker and Bob Tom Reed and drummer Jerry Barnett. The group played a countrified version of psychedelic rock and quickly gained a large following among the growing hippie culture of the time period.

The band played frequently at the Vulcan, which had quickly established itself as the premiere counterculture venue of the era. The venue featured many of the "out there" acts that were becoming popular at the time, famously hosting the legendary experimental New York City rock band the Velvet Underground in 1969. Jim Franklin recalls:

> *I did the posters for that show, and I went to dinner with them afterwards. Lou Reed asked me why didn't I use a more positive image in my poster. "Because we're a happy band." And I thought, well…I didn't say this, but…you've kind of got reputations for being junkies! In fact, you just finished doing that song, not even an hour ago, "I'm Waiting for My*

Man!" [laughs] *"Heeeeroiiiine!"* *"We're a happy band!"* Why did I use *a picture of a grave when your name is the* Velvet Underground! *I was afraid it was gonna be a little too obvious.*

The Vulcan also hosted many groups with heady band names that became in vogue in the wake of the Beatles' *Sgt. Pepper's Lonely Hearts Club Band*, groups such as Lord August and the Visions of Life, Space American Eagle Squadron, Strawberry Shoemaker and Sunnyland Special. In addition to booking the psychedelic "hippie" groups, the Vulcan also booked many traditional acts such as Big Mama Thornton, Muddy Waters, Freddie King and Lightnin' Hopkins. This combination of progressive and roots music represented an early trademark of Austin's musical legacy—steeped in tradition while simultaneously embracing more modern approaches to making music.

Shiva's Headband itself represented the nexus of these two axes. While the music it made was garage band–inspired psychedelic rock, its instrumentation prominently featured a fiddle, and for this reason its music had a decidedly country feel to it. Bill and Rim decided it would be the perfect band to record their third rock release, so they held a session during the daytime in the emptied-out Vulcan Gas Company.

The recordings were successful, producing the A-side "Kaleidoscoptic." However, the band and the label had an artistic difference of opinion concerning the song. While Shiva's Headband had wanted to record with the violin and guitars running through its amplifiers, as it was used to during live performances, Bill and Rim recorded using the "tapping" technique of running the instruments directly into the recording console. This was done partly to produce a cleaner sound but also partly out of necessity: tapped instruments meant that fewer microphones were needed, and microphones were still somewhat of a luxury for Sonobeat at the time. In any case, the band actually ended up being unhappy with the cleaner sound, and the single was never released. Instead, Bill and Rim decided to release a single by another popular local underground band known as the Conqueroo.

The Conqueroo, along with Shiva's Headband, was one of the most popular "underground" bands in Austin at the time. As such, it was also a popular mainstay at the Vulcan. The two bands had co-headlined the venue's grand opening on October 27 and 28, 1967. While the Conqueroo didn't share Shiva's countrified instrumentation, it did write and perform melodic, eclectic rock songs that fit in well with the counterculture crowd. The band consisted of guitarists Charlie Pritchard and Bob Brown, drummer Gerry Storm and multi-instrumentalist Ed Guinn. Guinn recalls:

It was a very sort of nascent scene; it was not unlike what you might find in a lot of small college towns in that time. There were kind of frat bands that had enough skill and discipline to play stuff that was popular for dancing at a lot of the parties and whatnot. And some of the clubs that catered to college kids. And we tended to be a lot more outside than that and not terribly accessible for the party scene. So it was, you know, fairly...I guess the scene was, as they often are, but maybe not so much anymore, very multi-leveled and separate. We didn't do stuff...we didn't play places where another band played. And the Gas Company tended to be a place where anybody could play, which is one of the reasons we were there so much. Because the stuff that we did wouldn't really play at the Jade Room, you know. And the Elevators had a touch and a groove that sort of bridged both the sort of outside experimental odd stuff and the more focused kind of party, poppy band scene. They fit in between both those things. We didn't. But it was, you know, it was a small scene and a few bands, and the Gas Company was a great place and a great idea. It showed real forward thinking, musically, in terms of what they were trying to do.

Bill Josey Sr. remembers:

We wanted to give the city and the region variety. Not all the same kind, but some kind of variety in music. And the Conqueroo was a group that was interesting to work with. They had Charlie Pritchard on lead, who was an excellent lead player, and of course they had Ed Guinn, who played flute, bass and keyboard. It was a versatile group.

The Conqueroo had come to prominence by opening shows for the 13th Floor Elevators, as well as hosting headlining gigs of its own around town. Bill and Rim regularly attended shows at the Vulcan Gas Company as a way to find new acts to record, and it was there during a Conqueroo gig that they offered to record the band in late 1967.

Again, recordings took place at the emptied-out Vulcan, with one session being held in December '67 and another in March of the following year. Ed Guinn recalls:

For us, it seems that the sessions were obviously a lot less formal than recording experiences subsequent to that. But I think that was the first thing we ever recorded as a band. I mean, aside from friends having little decks around and whatnot. So any studio stuff that came after that was much more formal, like you'd expect. You know, very rigid. I think, as I remember, Bill just said, "Go ahead and play your tune." And I think maybe we got levels…honestly I don't remember. But we played and did a few things. Our sessions were pretty easy, comfortable. The room sounded pretty awful. I was less than impressed by the boom, the crashiness, but I think it turned out pretty well. It certainly captured what we were doing.

The sessions ultimately resulted in the fifth Sonobeat release, stereo single R-s103 "I've Got Time," backed with "1 to 3." Both of the songs were originals, and both are a good example of the unique sound that was coming

Sonobeat single R-s103 "I've Got Time." *Courtesy of Sonobeat Historical Archive. Photo by Belmer Wright and artwork and lettering by Gilbert Shelton.*

out of Austin at the time. The record's sleeve featured psychedelic-tinged artwork by prolific Austin artist Gilbert Shelton.[13]

As with previous Sonobeat releases, "I've Got Time" sold well around town and helped widen the Conqueroo's fan base. The single would prove to be the only commercial release ever issued in the United States by the venerated Conqueroo (a compilation album was released in England in 1987). Nonetheless, the band retains a strong reputation and a solid fan base to the present day; a remaining copy of the "I've Got Time" single was recently listed on eBay for $125.

For the next release, Sonobeat would delve further into the realm of psychedelic rock. In late 1967, Bill and Rim had recorded a road-worn band of itinerant hippies called the Thingies. Originally from Topeka, Kansas, the band had already released a single on Casino Records before relocating to Miami, Florida. After a brief stint in the Sunshine State, it headed west, stopping on an extended layover in Austin. Bill Josey Sr. remembers:

> *They were originally from Florida and were on their way to California and stopped in Austin. The singer was Phil Weaver, and he stuttered very badly. But when he sang, he just sang as smooth as glass. They had a good light show, and you could go in any club that they were performing at, either early or late, and you'd see that* nobody *was leaving.*

Heavily influenced by bands like the Doors and the Elevators, the Thingies had quickly made a name for themselves with their spaced-out blend of jazz and rock-and-roll, along with their cryptic song lyrics. They had recorded a session with Bill and Rim at the Swinger's Club in December '67; the result was the single "Mass Confusion," backed with "Rainy Sunday Morning," released in the spring of 1968.

The single proved to be another critical success, and the buzz continued to build for the band. Unfortunately, as with the Elevators, the band was plagued with bad management. The group disbanded only months after the single's release. As with the Conqueroo, the band is still highly revered in small musical circles; its surviving 45rpm singles remain highly sought-after items among devoted record collectors.

In March 1968, Bill and Rim recorded and released the Lavender Hill Express's second single, the Rusty Wier–penned "Watch Out," backed with guitarist Leonard Arnold's "Country Music's Here to Stay." While the A-side maintains the driving '60s rock sound established with the group's first single, the B-side—as implied by the title—underscores the shift toward country-rock that was beginning to take place in popular music at the time. Leonard Arnold recalls:

> *I wrote that song after listening to "Nashville Cats" by the Lovin' Spoonful. They were a New York group. They cut that song, and it was a big surprise, because nobody expected a New York rock band to do a country song. But the fact is that even in those days those guys playing country music were way good. If you listen to ["Nashville Cats"], you'll hear the lyrics about how good the guitar players are at the beginning. That song inspired me to write "Country Music."*

As Arnold remembers, the shift to country music came about naturally for the band:

> *Rusty was doing all that early '60s R&B stuff. Before those days, most of the bands that were in Austin were country bands. And he played drums in some of those bands and sang in some of those bands, so he had the country groove going, I guess you could call it, before. But he wanted to play rock. And I had kind of started in the country scene, too. Rusty and I both had a lot of country in our upbringing, and I guess that was part of it. I guess Rusty and I had a lot to do with the country feel of the Lavender Hill Express, even though we were supposed to be a psychedelic band. We were doing Byrds music, which is basically just a rocked-up country music.*

The song featured country instrumentation: pedal steel guitar, acoustic rhythm guitar, drums, bass and a warbling lead vocal. This fit right in line with recent releases of the time period. Bob Dylan had released *John Wesley Harding* only three months before; the Gram Parsons–led International Submarine Band released *Safe at Home* the same month as the Lavender Hill Express single. The Byrds' seminal *Sweetheart of the Rodeo* would be released five months later. Arnold recalls:

> *We did those sessions at the Vulcan Gas Company, right on Congress Avenue. I remember we were cutting a song of Rusty's and a song of mine and one of Johnny Schwertner. We wanted some pedal steel on "Country Music's Here to Stay," so we called a guy in. I got to be friends with the guy, and that's how I got into playing pedal steel. I had to get one after that.*

The inclusion of "Country Music's Here to Stay" also foreshadows Austin's progressive rock movement that would rise to prominence in the mid-'70s. One of the originators and prominent figures of this movement would prove to be Lavender Hill Express drummer Rusty Wier, who would later switch from playing drums to fronting his own band. Arnold says:

> When we started the Lavender Hill Express, everybody was wearing Nehru shirts and trying to look British. That was the look everybody wanted to do. And somewhere along the line I started wearing a cowboy hat and cowboy boots and western shirts. Not that I was the only guy doing it, but for our band it was funny, because one night on break at the Jade Room Rusty and Jess wanted to have a little meeting with me. So we went out to the van, and they said, "Listen, man, you're starting to look a little bit too weird [laughs]. We don't want that look, we don't want that image." And the funny thing is, it wasn't long after that Rusty Wier started wearing a cowboy hat and never took it off again!

The release of "Watch Out/Country Music Is Here to Stay" was accompanied by a sly marketing technique. The sleeve featured a different cover on each side so that record stores could sell them in both the rock and country sections. The single earned the label and the band another positive review as a "Newcomer Pick" in the June 20 issue of *Cash Box* magazine, which described the song as "a powerhouse single that borrows from many, but imitates none" and having "a rock feel that should captivate top 40 listeners, and enough strength to score breakout sales."

Bill and Rim sent copies of the review along with each promo copy they sent out to radio stations and industry publications. Once again, the single sold well for an independent release, further increasing the band's and the label's statures in the local music scene, but as with previous attempts, the coveted major label deal proved to be too elusive.

In many ways, Sonobeat Records' commercial shortcomings early on in its existence played as important a role in the formation of the music scene as did its later successes. Because Sonobeat never became a goliath record label with dozens of household-name artists selling millions of records, each release would gain a sense of allure that comes with limited quantity and availability.

Sonobeat did just enough for the Austin music scene to galvanize Austin musicians without creating a commercial hub that would inundate the city with its own industry. In this way, Austin was able to build a reputation as a music town relatively free of the restraints of over-commercialization.

Later that year, Sonobeat Records issued its first LP, a ten-song, full-length jazz album by the Lee Arlano Trio titled *Jazz to the 3rd Power* that expanded on the previous year's single. The album was another critical success and featured the first album cover designed by Austin artist Jim Franklin.[14]

In May 1968, the Josey family moved into a considerably larger split-level house on Western Hills Drive in northwest Austin. The house featured a large bedroom/bath suite on the ground level and was a natural space to set up a home studio. Additionally, very little of northwest Austin had been developed in those days, giving the studio a sense of isolation and escape from the bustle of city life. Now that Bill Sr. had a room he could use as a studio at any time, he decided to invest more heavily in recording equipment. That summer, Sonobeat acquired its first half-inch four-track recorder, a Scully 280. The Scully gave Bill and Rim a much-needed technological improvement, allowing them to record with more clarity and efficiency.

Bill and Rim also designed and built a new portable ten-input mixer, as well as a steel plate reverb. The steel plate reverb was and remains an inventive, budget-friendly way to get a unique echo sound. A large sheet of steel (in the case of Sonobeat, five by nine feet) is connected with several rows of springs to a steel frame. The plate is driven by a transducer attached to the center of the plate, which in turn is driven by an amplifier. It is then set up in a different room than the singers and instruments, and the resulting motion of the plate from the sound waves is picked up by a set of microphones, through which it is added to the dry signal at the mixer. The steel plate reverb allowed Bill and Rim to simulate the sound of a large concert hall, all in the space of their tiny home studio.

"I remember we did another set of sessions out at Bill's place after he got his big reverb plate built," recalls former Lavender Hill Express guitarist Leonard Arnold. "It was a big ol' sheet of steel mounted on springs. And it sounded great. Nobody's ever come close to that reverb sound."

Bill's ongoing interest in recording technology had led to the construction of his home studio on Western Hills Drive. With added capabilities in the new recording space, he was eager to bring in the next act.

For their next recording project, Bill and Rim turned their attention to a completely different style of music, yet one that also fit into their eclectic sense of taste. The Afro-Caravan was a percussion-based jazz-rock band that brought a brand-new sound and style to the Austin music scene. The group was formed around Wali King, a New York City native who had studied African drumming and had even performed as a teenager at the 1964 New York World's Fair.

At the World's Fair, King had met Nigerian drummer and recording artist Babatunde Olatunji, a key figure in the roots revival happening in New York at the time. Olatunji encouraged King to continue to pursue his study of African music, and when he joined the armed forces two years later, he brought his drums with him. King's training as a military photographer eventually led him to Austin's Bergstrom Air Force Base.[15] King recalls:

> *I was born in the Bronx, New York City. I started studying African drumming up* [there] *in around 1964, but I've been in music in some capacity all my life, pretty much. I went into the service in 1966, did my basic training at Lackland Air Force Base in San Antonio. Basic training at that time was around six weeks, and then I ended up being in San Antonio for about six months awaiting assignment for a unit. So when my assignment finally came in, it was for Bergstrom. My stepfather was a professional photographer and a commercial artist, and I learned photography from him. So when I went into the service, I took the exam for being a photographer. I passed the exam and was accepted for on-the-job training. I went on leave first, and when I went on leave I decided to take my drums with me to Austin. By this time, I was into practicing as much as possible and studying music. I'd already been performing in New York City as a drummer, so I decided, you know, I'm gonna bring my drums with me. So I ended up, not knowing the type of equipment I was supposed to bring with me, instead of taking all the equipment I was assigned to bring to Bergstrom Air Force Base, I ended up leaving some of it at my house in the Bronx, and I used that space to pack my drums!* [laughs] *Which later on got me into a little bit of hot water because I didn't have some of the equipment I was supposed to have. I had to have my mother send me some stuff that I'd left at home, and I had to purchase some of the stuff that I'd left behind as well. So that wasn't a good start for me; my fist sergeant, he wasn't thrilled about that. And he didn't particularly care for people from New York; he had some kind of little…"Another one of these damn guys from New York!" He had kind of an attitude about that. So that's pretty much how I got to Bergstrom Air Force Base. That was around '66. I went into the service on March 31, and I think I got to Bergstrom like six months later. I was twenty-one.*

Wali became aware of Austin's growing music scene when some of the military personnel took note of his African-influenced drumming technique:

My introduction to the Austin music scene came when I finally got my assignment. I came down to Bergstrom, and I brought my drums with me. After I had my room assigned on base, I would practice my drums in the room. And then some of the airmen would hear me drumming, and they'd come and knock on the door and say, "Hey, what's going on?" And after a while people started coming in the room to hear me play. And so then first sergeant told me he didn't want me playing the drums in the barracks at certain times. So then someone told me we could go over to the Airmen's Club on the other side of the base. So I started going over to the Airmen's Club to practice my drums over there, and through playing the drums over there I started meeting a lot of the different airmen on the base. And some of the people started gravitating toward coming over when they knew I was gonna be there, and then eventually somebody invited me to bring my drums into the city. At first, it was just to hang out, but then they introduced me to some people. The black troops would go to a place called Ciro's. It was an all-night joint in one of the black areas of Austin. It was just a hangout spot, and that's where you meet and socialize with the local people. So I started developing friendships with people, and some of the people found out that I was a musician. So they would invite me, some people invited me over to the Huston-Tillotson campus to play drums over there. And I went over there, and I played…and I met some people who were interested in learning about the drums. And then somebody else brought me over to the University of Texas, where they had some of the black dormitories over there. They invited me to come into a couple of the dorm houses and play, and I met other people who were interested in learning about African music. So we started talking, and after a while I started teaching people, and we started getting together and hanging out in the park. And one of the guys who was at the University of Texas, he was also from Austin. And he said, "Well, we'll go to Zilker Park." So we started hanging out at Zilker Park when we had time off from the base. And we would drum over there, and then I met a couple of guys who played some other instruments, and we started creating some ideas about some music and stuff like that, and that's basically how I got started on the first round of things. They used to have "Love-Ins" at Zilker Park, and we got invited to play some Love-Ins and stuff like that. And I had had a group up in New York that I'd worked with that was called the Caravan. We needed a name, so I came up with the idea of Afro-Caravan. So we started performing under that name.

The band had a style and image that crossed racial and generational lines. Along with the Conqueroo and James Polk and the Brothers, the Afro-Caravan was one of Austin's first multiracial bands. It was equally at home performing at the east side's Afro Club as at the Vulcan Gas Company. As an African American from New York City, Wali had an outsider's perspective of Texas culture:

Oh, there was a big difference. Big difference. One of the things…I wasn't used to seeing civilians carrying guns. That was something that kind of struck me. Now, in Austin you didn't see as many people carrying guns as in other parts of Texas. Back then, they had the law that the weapon had to be exposed. So you saw a lot of people periodically that would have sidearms on 'em. And I just wasn't used to seeing that. Also, just the manner in which people handled themselves was a lot different. Austin was a lot different from other parts of Texas in terms of my experience there. There was a more liberal quality, I guess maybe because it was a university town. There was more of a liberal quality of live and let live there. You could get in some jams if you weren't careful, but I didn't have too many unusual incidents in Austin. And I felt like a lot of the well-traveled Texans were very nice and accommodating people. Every now and then you'd run into a little sample of racism, but I never ran into a lot of overt racism there. There was a certain level of institutional racism that was going on. Being in the wrong place at the wrong time, that kind of stuff. But other than that, it wasn't too bad. Because it was an LBJ town, there was kind of a thing, you know, "We're not gonna have that kind of thing here." Because with LBJ coming in behind Kennedy, and him being the person that was pushing all these Great Society things, Austin was kind of one of the places that felt like they were a direct representative of LBJ. And as a result of that, the town had much more of a liberal attitude, versus being in a town like San Marcos or something like that. Austin was kind of representing LBJ, and his local people kind of made sure it was a nice town for people. They didn't want any embarrassing situations to be coming up in Austin. So that kind of attitude was kind of there, and being a university town, the young folk weren't picking up what the old folk were doing; the majority of them were not interested in picking up that kind of segregated attitude. It was about, "Why can't we just get along? We need to find a way to get along…we have common causes, you know? The whole Vietnam era, we've ended up side-by-side fighting. Why should we be fighting in our own community?" That kind of thing, you know? A lot of that was happening in Austin, more so than, say, Houston, places like that.

The Afro-Caravan comprised students from the University of Texas, students from Huston-Tillotson University and personnel from Bergstrom Air Force Base. The unusual instrumentation of the original lineup consisted of King on percussion and vocals, Robert Moore as an additional percussionist, J. Murray on tenor and alto recorders, Ronald Nance on bass violin and Ray Lewis on the flute. Gigs around town led to on-air gigs on KAZZ, and eventually the group came to the attention of Bill Josey. King recalls:

> *They had a house band there* [at the Afro on East Eleventh Street] *that was run by a fellow named James Polk,*[16] *and they had a horn player there named "Wimp" Caldwell. And I used to hang out with both of those guys because they liked the sound the drum brought to the jazz pieces they were working on and some of the blues pieces. So they started asking me to come down and sit in with them. So that became a part of my thing when I had time off from the base. I would hang out with these guys and do some drumming with them, sit in with some of the local talent, stuff like that. And there was a fellow named D-Dawg. His real name is Emile Bolden, but he used to go by the name D-Dawg. He was a disc jockey for Bill Josey when Bill had that radio station. It was D-Dawg who invited me and some of my buddies to come to the radio station for an interview, and we played a little bit in the small radio station, and they got a response from the university, from Huston Tillotson; people really enjoyed it and started calling in. And Bill got the idea to do an on-site recording. This was around 1967.*

Shortly thereafter, Wali and the Afro-Caravan were given the opportunity to perform at HemisFair, the 1968 World's Fair held in nearby San Antonio. A six-month event scheduled from April to October, HemisFair was the first official World's Fair to be held in the southwestern United States. A ninety-two-acre swath of land on the southeastern edge of downtown San Antonio was almost completely demolished and redeveloped for the exposition. In its stead, developers built HemisFair Park, along with the 750-foot-high Tower of the Americas, which remains the tallest and most prominent figure in the San Antonio skyline. King remembers:

> *I met a fellow named Jim Wharton; he was the entertainment director for HemisFair, and he approached us about working there. The first time we worked HemisFair, it was a washed-out deal. We worked two days, and we rotated two performances with another group called Sweet Smoke out*

of San Antonio. They were an electric rock group, and they used to do this thing where they had a fog machine and the smoke would come out as they were making their music. So we would alternate...I forgot the actual place we played in the HemisFair because they had different sites where groups were performing at [sic]. But after the success of that initial weekend, Jim Wharton later on approached me about doing weekends down there. So on the weekends when I was free, we ended up performing at HemisFair. Friday night we'd truck on down and work there, then come back to Austin.

Bill and Rim agreed to record the band during a live performance at HemisFair in San Antonio. They recorded the set on a two-track Ampex 354 with a portable recording console and used two songs from the performance—"Comin' Home Baby" and "Afro-Twist"—as the band's first single.

"The 'Afro-Twist' got very popular around town, people really liked it," remembers Wali King. "So they started calling us for more work, and we ended up having a little mini-tour circuit around Austin."

The single proved to be another critical success and yet another excellent example of the eclecticism found in Austin music at the time. It also proved to mark the beginning of a fruitful relationship between the Afro-Caravan and Sonobeat Records. Interested in the band's unique sound and commercial potential, Bill offered to record the band's debut full-length album.

Ultimately, the project was delayed somewhat so that Bill and Rim could make time for what would prove to be the label's most successful record. During the recording sessions with the Conqueroo, Bill and Rim had the opportunity to sit in on a rehearsal session for an up-and-coming hotshot blues guitarist and singer/songwriter out of Beaumont. His name was Johnny Winter, and he would go on to provide Sonobeat with its first bona fide hit.

Mean Town Blues

Johnny Winter

Johnny Winter was born in Beaumont, Texas, in February 1944. Showing obvious musical talent from an early age, Winter and his brother, Edgar, were playing gigs from as young as ten, when the two performed a set of Everly Brothers songs for a local children's television show.

The Winter brothers were impossible to forget because of their unique sound and unique look; not only were they highly proficient blues multi-instrumentalists, but they both happened to be albino as well. By fifteen, they had formed a band and were playing regularly enough to cut the single "School Day Blues" for Houston's Big Beat label.

Around the same time, Johnny and Edgar got to see performances by touring blues legends such as Muddy Waters, B.B. King and Bobby Bland. Johnny even got to sit in on a major label recording session with Roy Head and the Tramps, cutting the single "Tramp" in 1967.

Johnny's rising profile led to more and more gigs throughout the region. He and his band toured throughout the South, but it turned out to be a series of gigs in Colorado that led to regular bookings in Austin at the Vulcan Gas Company. Jim Franklin recalls:

> *The Vulcan had been open for maybe a year. It opened in '67, closed in '70. And in '68, I think it was, it kind of acquired the attention of Johnny Winter. In San Francisco, the Family Dog was the beatnik-hipster organization that ran the Avalon Ballroom and did a lot of the music posters. It was instrumental in bringing Janis Joplin out to join up with*

Big Brother. Well, they opened up a venue in Denver called the Denver Dog. So it was a pretty bold step, you know, to split up their interest and have one [venue] halfway across the country. But they were doing so well in San Francisco that they could cross over. So one of the gigs at the Denver Dog was a guy from Houston, Johnny Winter, who we didn't know about 'cause he didn't play in Austin at that time. And he had a completely different kind of lifestyle; he was more of a Beatles mod. Haircut and everything. And it's well depicted on the cover of the Sonobeat album [The Progressive Blues Experiment]. So the Conqueroo was booked with Johnny Winter, and some of our guys from the Vulcan drove up to Denver with the band for the gig. And while they were there they got to meet Johnny Winter, and they were very impressed. Johnny had just had his trio for about a month, and he was planning to go to San Francisco and become discovered. But our guys persuaded him to come back to Austin. Guaranteed him a steady stream of gigs at the Vulcan so they could get their sound a little more refined, get it in better shape to go west, or [to] Nashville or wherever.

Johnny and his band came to the attention of Sonobeat Records during Bill and Rim's recording session with the Conqueroo at the Vulcan. Recognizing the young musician's potential, they offered to do a recording session. Johnny agreed. Frankline remembers:

It was during that time that Johnny was doing regular gigs at the Vulcan that this idea of doing an album with Sonobeat came about. Those guys were part of the early wave of people who realized what the future of the Austin scene was gonna be. They were certainly not unique—we all kind of sensed that we were the next Asheville or even the next San Francisco. So they made a deal, I guess Bill Josey of Sonobeat made a deal with Johnny Winter to record an album, and they decided to record it at the Vulcan during the off hours. And I projected a light show so they got the feeling of being at a gig. So I was there for the whole recording session, it went on for a couple of days. But it was very impressive, the quality of the recording and the playing. Johnny knew what he was doing.

The sessions took place during the daytime in the emptied-out club. Though the band plays "live," there is no audience aside from Bill, Rim and Vulcan artist-in-residence Jim Franklin. Johnny's backing band at the time consisted of "Uncle John" Turner on drums and Tommy Shannon on bass.[17]

The musicians performed in a tight circle in the center of the Vulcan's cavernous hall, with half a dozen dynamic and condenser microphones capturing the band up close while an additional microphone picked up the echo from the back of the room. All of the basic tracks were mixed "live" into a custom two-track Ampex 354 recorder. To set the mood, Franklin set up a psychedelic-influenced light show. Jon Inmon recalls:

> *Really the big breakout for Bill Josey was that live record of Johnny Winter's that he recorded at the Vulcan Gas Company. And it was one of my favorite records at the time; I wore that thing out. I wish I still had it! It's just a magnificent piece of work. And recently, in the last couple of years, I saw Tommy Shannon, and I said, "Do you remember that record you guys made at the Vulcan Gas Company?" He stopped what he was doing and looked right at me and said, "Man, that was the best record we made." And I gotta say I agree. It's just a mighty piece of work.*

Tommy Taylor adds:

> *I think that's Johnny's best record ever, and I think it's one of the best-documented events. I mean, it couldn't have been captured any better. It's kind of a little miracle, really, because if you were ever in the Vulcan Gas Company...the room had a very unique sound. It had a chemical sort of sound to it, and it's captured perfectly in that record. The natural reverb on that record is exactly what the Vulcan Gas Company sounded like. And it's such a miracle that we have that captured because it could have very easily just have been blown off. But that's what that room sounded like, and the recording is brilliant. It's a fantastic record.*

The session yielded eight tracks, and two more acoustic numbers were recorded in the living room of the Josey residence on Western Hills Drive in northwest Austin. Sonobeat chose to release a single first, issuing Winter's take on McKinley Morgenfield's blues standard "Rollin' and Tumblin'" on the A-side, backed with Johnny's original "Mean Town Blues." The sleeve features a ghostly black-and-white picture of Johnny, with sparse surrounding artwork designed in-house by Rim Kelley.

The single generated significant buzz, and shortly thereafter, Sonobeat issued a noncommercial "advance" pressing of the ten-song album in order to interest radio stations, publications and, most importantly, major record labels. In October of that year, Johnny visited the UK to check out the music scene. While there, he met the Vernon Brothers, owners of a successful UK blues label. He played them the advance copy of the record, and by the following month, Bill Josey had entered into negotiations for the licensing of the album, titled *The Progressive Blues Experiment*, to Blue Horizon for distribution in the UK, Europe and Canada.

When Johnny returned home in December, *Rolling Stone* magazine ran a feature article about musicians in Texas. Doug Sahm appeared on the cover, and the article raved about established rock stars such as Janis Joplin, Steve Miller and Mother Earth.[18] However, the article's writers reserved their most lavish praise for the young, as-yet-unknown albino guitar player from Beaumont:

> *The hottest item outside of Janis Joplin, though, still remains in Texas. If you can imagine a hundred and thirty pound cross-eyed albino with long fleecy hair playing some of the gutsiest fluid guitar you have ever heard, then enter Johnny Winter. At 16, Bloomfield called him the best white blues guitarist he had ever heard. Now 23, Winter has been out and around for some time…In addition to guitar, Winter also plays superb harp and has a fine hard blues voice. His visual and audible presence is a subtle parallel to Joplin's.*

Seemingly overnight, things started happening. Johnny and his band left for New York City, where Johnny had been asked by Mike Bloomberg to sing and play a song during one of his concerts at the Fillmore East. Representatives for Columbia Records were in attendance, and Johnny did not disappoint. Within a few days, Johnny had signed a multimillion-dollar contract with a $600,000 advance—purportedly the largest in the history of show business at the time.

Meanwhile, Sonobeat ceased negotiations with Blue Horizon and instead sold the rights to *The Progressive Blues Experiment* to Liberty Records. The Josey family made the drive all the way out to Los Angeles to hand deliver the master tapes to Liberty president Bud Dain. Jack Josey remembers:

> *It wasn't long after moving to the new house that the Sonobeat deal to sell the Johnny Winter album was concluded with Liberty Records. The photo taken of me sitting on the piano bench with Johnny Winter was in our living room. I wasn't as impressed with Johnny Winter's music as my father and brother were—mainly because I didn't like his singing voice. Plus, Johnny Winter was a blues guy and I was, as a young teen, a top*

40 music fan. I was too young and immature musically to see that Johnny was on his way to something really big. My dad, on the other hand, had the knack—and perhaps great luck—to find talented musicians. Johnny Winter's success was almost overnight. It's as if the music industry was waiting for something totally different than what was being played on top 40 radio at the time. The most vivid memory I have of Johnny is when I went with my dad to Austin's Robert Mueller Municipal Airport to either pick Johnny up or drop him off—I can't remember which. My dad, Johnny Winter and I sat in my dad's white T-Bird for about a half an hour as I passed Johnny numbered white albums to autograph. He signed number ninety-six for me. I remember Johnny as a soft-spoken person, whereas my father had a slightly southern radio voice and was usually the one doing most of the talking in any conversation. So the scene I remember is my dad telling Johnny what to write on each of the albums.

Doug Hanners, a longtime Austin record collector, music journalist[19] and music historian, recalls that selling a master tape to a major label was, as it is today, extremely rare at the time:

It was a big deal in those days for a little label like Sonobeat to get picked up and distributed, you know, sell a master to the big guys like that. It had happened in Austin back in the '50s with some 45s, but it wasn't common at all. That was the Domino label and the Slates. But there weren't many that got a break into the big time like they did.

In May of the following year, Liberty Records released the album on its subsidiary, Imperial Records. The album beat the Columbia release, simply titled *Johnny Winter*, to shelves by two weeks, peaking at number forty-nine on the Billboard charts in April '69. Johnny was a certified rock star, and Sonobeat had hit its first payday.

Johnny Winter and his younger brother, Edgar, both went on to long and successful careers in the music industry, recording and releasing over sixty albums between the two of them over the next four decades. Meanwhile, Sonobeat forged ahead with its business operations, releasing a string of new singles in the wake of its success.

First off was the country-western single "Can't Win for Losing," backed with "Windy Blues," by local honky-tonkers Ronnie and the West Winds. Also recorded at the Vulcan, the single marks the first (and only) foray into the country-western genre, further underscoring Sonobeat's wide diversity. The single received airplay on KOKE-FM and sold moderately well throughout central Texas.

Bill and Rim followed up their country release with something completely different. In 1968, the United States was in its third year of full-on combat operations in the Vietnam War. Along with the civil rights movement, this was one of the most highly charged topics in a politically turbulent era. In 1965, just as the first U.S. combat units were being deployed, a young Vietnamese jazz singer named Bach Yen was booked for a two-week visit to New York as a musical emissary for South Vietnam. She appeared as a musical guest on *The Ed Sullivan Show*, and incredibly, her stay in America expanded from two weeks to almost twelve years.

Yen had been performing in Saigon nightclubs from an early age. Her repertoire included songs in English, French, Spanish, Italian and Hebrew, as well as her native Vietnamese. In 1961, she moved to Paris, seeking a career as an international jazz singer in the vein of Edith Piaf. In France, she recorded several albums for Polydor records and toured Europe for several years but was constantly at odds with the label, which wanted her to adopt a more contemporary style and image. In 1965, she received the invitation to perform on *The Ed Sullivan Show* and decided to try her luck in the American market.

During her twelve-year residency in the United States, Yen performed in forty-six states, as well as Canada, Mexico and several other Latin American countries. She appeared frequently on national television, with guest performances on variety shows hosted by Bob Hope, Bing Crosby, Joey Bishop, Mike Douglas and Pat Boone. She also toured in package shows with artists such as Frankie Avalon, Jimmy Durante and Liberace.

In 1968, she made arguably one of the most controversial moves in her career, singing on the soundtrack to John Wayne's right-wing film *The Green Berets*. While the gig gave her more public exposure than ever before, it also drew criticism from some of her fans back home.

The movie did, however, introduce Yen and her music to Cactus Pryor. Already a legendary figure in Austin broadcasting, Pryor got his start covering local news on President and Lady Bird Johnson's radio station 590 KLBJ. Eventually, he switched over to television, broadcasting for local Austin station KTBC (also owned by the Johnsons). His popularity as a humorist and broadcaster led to appearances in two of John Wayne's movies: *Hellfighters* and *The Green Berets*.[20]

Pryor was particularly impressed by Yen's musical talents, and during their time on set, he invited her to perform at his friend Don Dean's Club

Seville in Austin. It was here that Bill agreed to hold a recording session in January 1968. The two-hour session yielded the basic tracks to Sonobeat single PV-s109. Side A featured the Charlie Chaplin–penned "This Is My Song," while side B showcased Yen's rendition of the French jazz number "Magali." The Club Seville's house band, the Michael Stevens IV, provided the instrumental backing.

Though initial sessions were held in January, Bill delayed the release of the single, feeling that the backing track needed a richer sound. In the meantime, things started to get busy with other recording projects (namely Johnny Winter's), and Yen's recording kept getting pushed back. Finally, in August, Josey hired Richard Green and members of the Austin Symphony Orchestra to arrange and perform an overdubbed string and horn section for the two tracks. The songs were completed, and the single was released in October.

Though Yen's single was not a huge commercial success, it did provide the singer with one of her first American recordings while also adding international intrigue to the Sonobeat label. Yen would eventually return to Paris in 1977, becoming professionally and romantically involved with the Vietnamese multi-instrumentalist and ethnomusicologist Tran Quang Hai. Under Hai's tutelage and influence, the two began to focus on traditional Vietnamese music, learning traditional instruments such as the dan tran zither and singing in their native tongue. The duo went on to release seven albums and continued to perform in concerts throughout the world.

Throughout the late 1960s and the early '70s in America, the Vietnam War served as a looming specter in the background, a hemisphere away but at the same time all too close to home. Kids coming of age during the time period had been aware of the conflict since its Cold War roots in the mid-1950s. Despite widespread opposition, the United States had become more involved with each successive president, from Eisenhower to Kennedy to Johnson, and an increasing number of American teenagers were being sent to risk their lives fighting for a cause that many of them cared little about.

The Tet Offensive had been launched by the Viet Cong in January 1968, shocking the American public and demonstrating that the communist-backed North Vietnamese army was much more resilient and capable than previously imagined. Suddenly, the American government had less credibility with its citizenship, especially the younger generation, which was increasingly being asked—then ordered—to fight in its name.

In March, President Johnson declared that he would not seek reelection. Three months later, the leading Democratic candidate, Robert F. Kennedy, was assassinated in Los Angeles. The murder of another political hero, along with the assassination of civil rights activist Martin Luther King Jr. in April, led to one of the most turbulent, violent protests in the nation's history at the Democratic National Convention, held in Chicago late in August of that year.

Rock musicians, of course, were caught right in the eye of the storm; they were the embodiment of the antiwar counterculture, yet if they were not exempted, deferred or disqualified, they often became victims of involuntary conscription. This would only increase in the coming years of the Nixon administration and with the implementation of the draft lottery late in 1969. Tommy Taylor remembers:

> It was heavy, man. The war had been going on for a long time. Our whole thing as junior high school students was, "Oh, shit, man, we've got about three years, and then our number comes up." Musicians were getting drafted right and left. People were doing anything they could do because…I mean, most musicians aren't really into war. It kind of just goes against art. But a lot of cats were called for the draft. A lot of guys were joining the service so they wouldn't be drafted so they might be able to get a gig in the band. "Oh shit, well if I'm gonna get drafted…I mean, if I just join, I'm a good enough player, I can get in the band and then I won't be marching in Vietnam." But other cats freaked. One of my dearest mentor/friends, Thurston Mannex, is a brilliant guitarist, probably one of the best Austin ever knew, and nobody will ever even know who he is. He was a little older than Eric Johnson and kind of mentored Eric, he kind of helped Eric along when he was real young. The guy was an unbelievable guitar player. But Thurston got drafted, and while he was away they stole his [Gibson ES] 335, his guitar. And he never played again. He came back from the war, and that was it; they stole his guitar, and he didn't play guitar any more. It's a real drag because the guy was on his way to becoming something really fantastic, something really major. I mean, he was world-class talent, and the war just preempted his destiny there. "Sorry, you're gonna go to Vietnam." And then he never played again, to my knowledge.

The war was having more and more of a negative effect on the American youth, which in turn galvanized the antiwar counterculture movement. Through it all, Sonobeat continued to produce records and capture the sounds of a rapidly changing world.

Between the completion of the Bach Yen single in August 1968 and its release in October of the same year, Rim Kelley produced and engineered the third and final Lavender Hill Express single for Sonobeat Records.

"Outside My Window," an experimental rock song by Layton DePenning, was chosen as the A side, while Rusty Wier's acoustic ballad "Silly Rhymes" constitutes Side B.

During the sessions, a third song was recorded and intended as the A side of Lavender Hill Express's fourth single; however, the band broke up shortly after an ill-fated three-week residency gig in Phoenix. Nevertheless, each of the individual members had long, influential careers in the music business. Leonard Arnold remembers:

> *In the Lavender Hill, Rusty was the guy. He was the main singer. But I can tell you this about Rusty Wier, and I told both of his boys the same thing, so you can print this: Rusty was just about the worst drummer I ever played with [laughs]. He didn't even use a high-hat. He didn't have one! But he was a singer out there playing drums. All it was, Rusty was a good drummer, a lot of fun and a showman for sure, but he would speed up when he was doing fills. He'd start at the high tom, and by the time he got to the floor tom, he was going almost twice as fast. In other words, he couldn't fill without getting out of meter, which is one of the reasons why, after we broke up the Lavender Hill, he went and got a guitar. I think somebody gave him some advice, and I think it was good advice. 'Cause for one thing, he's a front man, and it's really hard to be a front man when you're on the drums. At the Jade Room, it worked pretty good 'cause there was a drum-riser down there and you could see him really well. But most of the time, the drummer's behind somebody. So Rusty became a guitar player, and that's when he became Rusty Wier. He was already pretty popular around Austin in those days. He's always had the personality and the charisma. That stupid grin [laughs]. He wasn't a great singer; he could just deliver a song and make everybody believe.*

Tommy Taylor adds:

> *Rusty, he was the first person to have a real standout persona in Austin. I can't really say enough about Rusty; he was just one of those people who stood out. He had that Elvis sort of charisma, you know. People just were drawn to him; he made you feel comfortable, and he entertained you. A lot of people were musicians, but there's a difference.*

Rusty Wier and Layton DePenning joined guitarist John Inmon and became a folk-rock trio known as Rusty, Layton and John. The band drew major label interest, but no deal was ever made. Eventually, Wier would sign a deal as a solo artist and maintain a career that spanned nine albums and three decades.[21] A beloved Austin entertainer, he passed away from cancer in 2009. Arnold recalls:

> *You know, Rusty, Layton and John, those are three of my favorite humans that I've known in my life. Later on, they went with him, they called it Rusty, Layton and John. They didn't have a drummer, but every now and then they did—a guy named Donny Dolan who's from Temple. And me and Gary P. played with Michael Martin Murphy for a while, and then I worked with Steve Fromholz for several years there, too. But during that time, we were living in this house out in the country, they called it the "Hill on the Moon." And we had our band set up in the living room all the time; we could play all day. It had everything we needed out there. But we all lived out there together, those three guys, me, Layton, John and Donny Dolan. Gary P. had a room out there, and he moved out and asked me if I wanted it, and I said I'll take it. I'd been looking for a place to live, and here was an opportunity to live with three of my favorite musicians! So we lived out there for around three years, and everybody went through that place. Jerry Jeff, Michael Murphy, Fromholz, Bobby Bridger, all that country-rock, redneck-rock stuff.*

Leonard Arnold formed the Austin rock trio Phoenix before moving to Nashville. Layton DePenning played with Rusty and then later with B.W. Stephenson; he currently owns and operates a recording studio in Buda, Texas, just south of Austin. Gary P. Nunn, who replaced Johnny Schwertner as keyboardist in 1968, went on to further local prominence as a member of Jerry Jeff Walker's Lost Gonzo Band.

The year 1968 continued to be a busy and prolific one for Sonobeat Records. In October, Rim engineered the first in a series of recording sessions with upcoming Austin hard rock band New Atlantis. Loaded with potential, the band featured virtuoso guitarist Jim Mings, along with keyboardist Mike Reid, drummer Jay Meade and former 13th Floor Elevator bassist Danny Gallindo. Bill Josey Sr. remembers:

> *I believe that the New Atlantis had more possibility, better possibilities of becoming something big of anyone [we] ever recorded. Rim and I had cut two sides before we went to LA in '69. We took these out there, and they played them, and they went, "Wow." And they wanted an album. And*

when I came back and talked to the New Atlantis about it, they decided to break up, which turned me every way but loose! I could not believe it. They had personality conflicts that they did not think they could resolve.

In addition to the band's Zeppelin-influenced, spaced-out sound, the single featured some impressive studio trickery courtesy of Rim Kelley. Bill Josey Sr. recalls:

Rim did something that I didn't even know what it was for a long time. On a mix down, he had made a very special kind of ring modulator [dubbed the "Sonotone Black Box"]. And he put this on Jim Ming's guitar on one side, and that was the Jimi Hendrix song "Fire." That's the most explosive sound...that's one that you really will have to hear. You won't believe it when you hear it. The guitar becomes an animal of the jungle. It has such a gutsy type of sound that everybody out in LA that heard this—Dino, who was the United Artist manager of their recording studio, he always wanted to know how in the world we got that sound.

In spite of the major-label interest, the New Atlantis recordings were never released. Sonobeat continued to produce records, issuing three more seven-inch singles before the end of the year.

The first was a novelty single by native Austin rockabilly artist Ray Campi. Campi had been in the music business since the early '50s, playing Saturday night jamborees at the Sportcenter on Barton Springs Road (the venue would later become the iconic Armadillo World Headquarters). For his session with Sonobeat, he recorded the self-penned sort-of protest song "Civil Disobedience," a tongue-and-cheek jab at the counterculture phenomenon occurring in American society at the time. Some example lyrics: "Civil Disobedience brings us free room and board/The best the jailhouse can afford" and "From the way we look it's hard to tell we're human."

The B side, titled "He's a Devil in His Hometown," features a vaudeville style and instrumentation, performed with Campi's natural tendency toward rockabilly. The resulting single was a mixed bag—radio stations weren't sure what to do with it, so it received little attention and sold poorly. Nonetheless, it further demonstrates Sonobeat's increasingly diverse catalogue of recordings and further paints a picture of the social currents of the era.

The next Sonobeat single featured two original compositions written by Herman M. Nelson, a longtime acquaintance of Bill Sr. Nelson had been writing poems and songs for years and, with the release of the single, became the first artist to write songs exclusively for Sonobeat's subsidiary publishing company, titled Sonosong Music. Those songs included the A-side "About to Be Woman," along with the B-side "Leaves," both of which local folksinger Jim Chesnut recorded for his Sonobeat single release.

Chesnut, a native of Midland, Texas, had also been a classmate of Rim Kelley's at the University of Texas. With the release of "About to Be Woman," Chesnut had his first commercial single, while Sonosong had its first catalogued compositions under its belt.

Shortly after recording the single, Chesnut recorded an entire album's worth of Nelson's tunes, creating Sonobeat's (and Sonosong's) first song demo album, *Songs from the Catalogue of Sonosong Music Company: Herman M. Nelson, Composer*. The "album" was recorded at the Josey residence with just vocals and a guitar and was not released commercially; instead, Bill sent copies to established record labels in hopes of getting one of the songs recorded by a major-label artist.

Chesnut continued to play gigs around Austin, and in May 1969, he returned to Sonobeat to record a handful of cover songs. Though the material was never released, his experience with Sonobeat foreshadowed his subsequent career in the music industry.

In the 1970s, Jim moved to Nashville and earned a position as a staff writer for the famed Acuff-Rose music publishing company. One of his compositions, "Show Me a Sign," earned a Grammy nomination in 1979. Chesnut also recorded a pair of albums and thirteen charting singles in the 1970s, playing in clubs from coast to coast between recording stints.

In the early 1980s, he retired from the music industry, returning to Texas. Today, he owns and operates an audiovisual and graphics production business in San Antonio and still plays locally from time to time. In 2008, he released *Reflections*, his first independent record in nearly three decades. *Sippin' Whiskey*, another new album, followed in 2012.

The final Sonobeat release of 1968 was a bossa-nova rendition of the Lennon/McCartney composition "Yesterday" by local jazz singer Fran Nelson. Backed by the same house band that had recorded with Bach Yen and Don Dean, the recording marked the end of what would prove to be Sonobeat's busiest and most productive year; all told, eleven singles and three full-length albums were recorded by Bill and Rim, all but one of which made their way onto record store shelves.

With each release, Sonobeat was establishing itself more and more as a driving force in the local music scene. Suddenly, musicians were becoming aware of Austin as a place where they could be commercially recorded. The label provided a small but significant avenue for local musicians to reach the next level of success; this, in turn, would set the table for the following decade, in which singer/songwriters such as Willie Nelson, Jerry Jeff Walker and B.W. Stephenson would bring attention to Austin as the center of the progressive country movement.

Sonosong was now a saleable entity, and recording had already commenced for what would be Sonobeat's third commercial album release. As with *The Progressive Blues Experiment* before it, the record would prove to be one of Sonobeat's defining achievements.

Number 1900 East Twelfth Street, January 1965. *PICA 17841, Austin History Center, Austin Public Library.*

Home Lost and Found

Throughout the excitement of Johnny Winter's success and the busy recording and release schedule that followed, Sonobeat maintained a strong interest in Wali King and the Afro-Caravan. Recording sessions for their debut full-length album commenced in the fall of 1968. Wali King recalls:

> We did [the album] *out at Bill Josey's house. The studio was down in the basement. He and his wife had a very beautiful house out on Balcones Drive. Very nice house. And Rim built the studio—he'd just tell Bill what he needed and then he'd put it all together. So we actually recorded in the basement studio. We did about maybe three sessions to lay down the material, then I went back to do a little overdub here and there on some of the work.*

The sessions yielded seven tracks, five of which were Afro-Caravan originals. The songs vary in length, some ranging as long as eleven minutes, giving the band ample opportunity to stretch out its sound.

By early 1969, the album was completed, and as with the Johnny Winter record before it, Bill printed up a series of "white jacket" releases in hopes of attracting major-label interest. Through the same connections at Liberty Records, Bill was again successful, selling the album's rights for major-label distribution. King remembers:

One of the times that we did the Vulcan Gas Company was with Johnny Winter. And Johnny Winter got discovered partly through working with Bill. Bill was working on recording Johnny Winter, and that's how Liberty got interested in what Bill was doing. So for the attraction to Liberty Records, we kind of came in on Johnny Winter's coattails on that. Because they were so impressed with Johnny Winter, they said, "Well, what else you got, Bill?" And Bill said, "Well, I just happen to have...something that's very different!" Because the whole thing about Johnny Winter in that time was, you know, he was an albino white guy playing the blues. And he was so amazing on the guitar, you'd say, "Wow." First of all, he's blind, and he's albino...this is something very interesting. So then Bill told them about us, and they were interested.

The album, titled *Home Lost and Found*, was released in 1970 on United Artists/Liberty Records' Solid State jazz label as SS-18065. The record garnered excellent reviews; however, it failed to make the same impact on the charts that *The Progressive Blues Experiment* had a year before. Part of the reason may have been due to the rapidly evolving musical landscape from the time period. King remembers:

I was thrilled about [the new album]. *The only thing that was unfortunate about my situation in terms of the recording was that it took a long time for Liberty to put it into development. And as a result of that, Santana came out, and they moved the whole Afro-sound experience off into the electronic field with their approach. See, we were coming from this acoustic approach, and that got the Liberty people kind of nervous because at that time they didn't know how far the rock was gonna go. They were saying, "Well, what's gonna be the music of tomorrow." And then they gradually realized for themselves businesswise that the money was in rock. So we kind of got caught up in them not pushing us as hard as they originally were going to do because they decided that they weren't going to put that much money into acoustic music; they were going to put more money into the development of the rock scene. And so as a result, even though we had a foldout cover,[22] it got to be a situation of "Hold up the press. How far are we gonna go with this when the electronic music is taking over the scene out here." Because Jimi Hendrix's music was selling like wildfire at the time. So it was like, "Well, maybe we're not going to put as much into this as we had hoped we were going to." And that's kind of what happened to it.*

86

Nonetheless, Liberty Records went ahead and released the album nationwide, initially focusing its promotional efforts on the East Coast. King continues:

> *The first pressing was something like 3,500, and they did a field testing on it. They found that it moved well in some of the urban areas. They used Philadelphia as one of the places, and it did very well in Philadelphia. But in other places, it was like the sleeper, so they decided not to put the budget that they had originally developed into it. So it kind of got lost after a while. I think that eventually it sold maybe 35,000 altogether across the country. I still run into musicians that tell me, "Man, I saw a copy of your album in the so-and-so bin!" [laughs] They'd go out and travel, and some of them, they are collectors of discs and stuff like that...I have a couple of musician friends that actually purchased a couple of copies that they found as they were traveling across the country. So it's been serving almost like a calling card for me through the years. [laughs] But I'm very proud of it. I'm very proud of what we did, and the work that Bill and Rim put into it. I have a lot of respect for Bill and for Rim in terms of the effort that they made on behalf of pulling the music together within us and working with us in the studio.*

The Afro-Caravan continued to play around town and would later record again with Sonobeat Records.

Compared to the previous year, 1969 was a relatively slow one for Sonobeat Records. Though Bill had had success with *The Progressive Blues Experiment* and *Home Lost and Found*, he had also spent considerable resources for all of Sonobeat's recording endeavors the previous year. Thus, the recording schedule in '69 was kept to a slower pace.

In August, Bill Josey held a session with an up-and-coming jazz-inflected rhythm-and-blues band called James Polk and the Brothers. Polk, who was born in Corpus Christi in 1940, would prove to be one of the most influential figures in the history of Austin's jazz scene. His band, which featured vocalist and songwriter Yvonne Joseph, played frequently at east side hotspots such as Charlie's Playhouse, Ernie's Chicken Shack and the Afro.

For the Sonobeat sessions, the group recorded two original compositions at the Joseys' home studio in northwest Austin. The songs would eventually be released as Sonobeat's seventeenth 45rpm single, "Stick-To-It-Tive-Ness," backed with the instrumental "The Robot."

The record straddles the line between jazz and R&B, with Joseph delivering a soulful, gospel-tinged vocal performance over Polk's trademark

Hammond organ phrasings. The rhythm and horn sections, consisting of drummer John Taylor, guitarist Tim Pickard, saxophonist Reginald Caldwell and trumpeter Donald Jennings, provide a tight groove for the soloists to stretch out upon, and the record's A side carries a simple, somewhat socially conscious message indicative of the time period:

> *Things may seem like they are down*
> *But someday soon there's going to be higher ground*
> *And no one can hurt you or reach you so high*
> *No one can harm you as long as you try to have stick-to-it-tive-ness.*

The song was heavily influenced by Aretha Franklin's enormous hit "Respect," released two years earlier. The recording also marks Sonobeat's first foray into the realm of soul/R&B, further emphasizing Sonobeat's marked eclecticism. As with Franklin's monumental work, the lyrics feature a socially conscious message, serving as a snapshot of the social currents of the time.

Shortly after recording the single, James Polk embarked on his own career as a producer, founding Twink Records later that year ("Twink" was the nickname of a friend of Polk's who owned the popular '60s East Side nightclub Hide-a-Way Lounge). In 1970, he returned to Sonobeat, recording an album's worth of material, but the record was never released.

Shortly thereafter, Polk got the biggest gig of his career, moving to Los Angeles to join the Ray Charles Orchestra. He performed with the R&B icon for the next ten years, touring the world and eventually serving as writer, arranger and conductor. In 1988, he moved back to Austin, earning his master of music degree at Southwest Texas State University in nearby San Marcos. He spent the better part of the next two decades teaching and today remains a highly influential figure in the Austin jazz scene.

The year 1969 also saw the release of the debut single from Austin rock band Plymouth Rock. Consisting of guitarist John Inmon, drummer Donny Dolan, bassist Bobby Shehorn and former Lavender Hill Express keyboardist Johnny Schwertner, the band was formed shortly after the breakup of the South Canadian Overflow, another one of the Austin college/hippie crowd's most popular acts. John Inmon recalls:

> *I came to Austin to play music at the end of '65. My father was a retired army doctor, and he took a job at Scott & White Hospital up in Temple. And I had been playing guitar already for several years. I played in a dinky*

*little surf band in San Francisco right before we moved here and started
playing in Germany, where we were stationed. And as soon as I got to
Temple, I had to have a band. I was just sort of a hopeless music junkie.
I lived and breathed it, and always have since I started. So I got a band
immediately, got in a band, formed one. So I was up there in Temple, and
as you can imagine, there were not a lot of places you could play in Temple
in 1965 as a teenager. So we'd just drive down to the nearest town; it cost
us a dollar at the time to fill up our cars…gas was like 15 cents a gallon.
And so we'd drive down to Austin, and we'd play frat parties and local
clubs like the Jade Room and the New Orleans Club, the Action Club,
places like that. The first band I played in was a band called the Reasons
Why, and we were just sort of a young cover band that was stretching our
wings trying to learn how to fly. But the serious guys stayed in and the
not-so-serious guys dropped out, eventually, as is the way with everything.*

When Inmon, Dolan and Shehorn left South Canadian Overflow and
joined up with Schwertner, they also brought much of their previous band's
fan base with them. They had a bona fide manager in the form of KNOW
disc jockey Paul Harrison, and every member of the group had already had
a working relationship with Bill and Rim (South Canadian Overflow had
recorded one of the early Sonobeat sessions back in 1967, but the recordings
were never released). Inmon continues:

*All these bands, it was all very incestuous. People quit bands, joined other
bands and would go hear each other play and all that kind of stuff. There
was a friendly competition, everybody was really nice to each other back
then; there wasn't a lot of knife-in-the-back bullshit going on. Everybody
was pretty happy, and there was plenty of work, and you could watch a lot
of good bands.*

For the Plymouth Rock sessions, Rim Kelley recorded the basic instrumental
tracks in the auditorium of the First Cumberland Presbyterian Church, where
he and his father had been longtime members. Additional overdubs were
recorded at the home studio on Western Hills Drive, and in October, Sonobeat
issued the single "Memorandum," backed with "Just a Start."

"Memorandum" marks a return to Sonobeat's focus on the driving
psychedelic rock popular with the youthful hippie culture of the time period.
As was the case with most recordings of this genre, Rim Kelley handled
production duties.[23]

As with previous Sonobeat rock releases, the Plymouth Rock single showcases strong musicianship and an experimental approach (particularly noticeable on the psychedelic-tinged intertwining double-guitar solo). "Memorandum" went on to become Sonobeat's most successful single of 1969.

Like so many of the musicians on Sonobeat's roster, the members of Plymouth Rock would later go on to considerable success in the music industry. After a short-lived stint in the prog-rock band Genesee, John Inmon would join Gary P. Nunn and Bob Livingston in Jerry Jeff Walker's Lost Gonzo Band, recording a string of highly successful national releases with Jerry Jeff (*Viva Terlingua, Ridin' High, A Man Must Carry On*), as well as six acclaimed releases under their own name.

Inmon, widely considered one of the best guitar players in Austin, still maintains a steady stream of gigs to this day. He has worked with some of the most popular names in Texas music, including Townes Van Zandt, Joe Ely, Ray Wylie Hubbard, Bruce Robison, Pat Green, Jimmy LaFave, Eliza Gilkyson, Jimmie Dale Gilmore, Delbert McClinton, Marcia Ball and Omar and the Howlers. He has also built a considerable career as singer and songwriter; his song "Railroad Man" remains a fan favorite from the Lost Gonzo Band's 1975 self-titled debut.

Seeking to duplicate the past success of Johnny Winter's *The Progressive Blues Experiment*, Bill and Rim began scouting musicians around Austin to form a "super-group" in the vein of the Lavender Hill Express. The first musician they recruited was a drummer from Austin named Vince Mariani. A virtuosic percussionist with a distinctive jazz-influenced rock style, Mariani had been working with several bands in Colorado but had recently returned to Austin. Tommy Taylor remembers:

> *Vince Mariani was an incredible drummer and probably one of the most creative people on the planet. And he was playing in local groups...he had a standing engagement at the Continental Club six nights a week. His father was a professor of art at the University of Texas up until a few years ago, he was a brilliant artist known worldwide. And Vince was doing very well. He played drums in the Austin High School band, but they didn't make him march. He was such an amazing drum set player; during the football games, they brought a stage out and set his drums up, and he played a drum solo. On the football field! He made the front page of the* Austin American-Statesman; *the guy was a mesmerizing player. And Josey recognized that.*

Inspired by Los Angeles session drummer Sandy Nelson, who had released a string of drum solo singles and whom the Joseys had had a chance to meet when they drove out to Los Angeles to deliver *The Progressive Blues Experiment* masters, Bill and Rim decided to cut a drum solo single with Mariani. Titled "Pulsar" and backed with the additional solo drum composition "Boots," the single showcased Mariani's prodigious drumming abilities as well as a light touch of studio trickery—Rim Kelley added a slight flange effect to the final mix to give it a psychedelic flourish.

As a solo drum single, the record already had a limited market. Though it was a commercial failure, the single helped to establish Mariani's name as one of the premier drummers in Austin. Now, Bill and Rim set out to help create a powerhouse band around him.

The first person to audition was referred through Vince himself, and for good reason. At only fifteen years old, Eric Johnson was already an electrifying guitar player. A prodigious musician from early childhood, he received his first guitar at age eleven and, in two years' time, was playing around town. Leonard Arnold recalls:

> *I can tell you a story about him. There was a guy in Austin named Walter Hutchison. He worked for Dan Strait over at Strait Music for a long time. Before he went to work there, he had a little store over off Twenty-ninth Street, and I worked for him for a while. It was during the time I was still with the Babycakes. But we were building speaker cabinets over there, and I was teaching guitar lessons and selling guitars. Anyway, one day a couple of young guys, twelve or thirteen years old, walked in the store, wanted to try out a guitar. So I got 'em all hooked up, plugged 'em in, got 'em an amp goin', gave him a guitar to play. And he started playing, and I couldn't believe how good the kid was. And it turns out that it was Eric Johnson, and that was the first time I ever met him. But I'll tell you this—that was a moment in my life when I realized early on that I was never gonna be anywhere near as good a guitar player as all these young guys are. [laughs] But that was a defining moment in my career. I went ahead and kept going because I was pretty good at steel then. But Johnson came in and blew my mind, and I have never been the same since.*

Johnson developed his phenomenal guitar skills through countless hours of practice. This was evident to future label mate Leonard Arnold when the two had a chance encounter several years earlier:

I guess that's all he did. I mean, I thought I practiced a lot when I was in high school. I didn't even start playing till I was a junior. And, well, by the time he was…well, he could have been older than twelve, I can't remember. He looked about twelve, but he still looks like he's about twelve, so I just don't know exactly how old he was at the time. But he couldn't have been more than fifteen or sixteen years old. And he had a friend with him, and I don't remember who that was, but man, I'll never forget that moment. I think there was a 330, and a little Fender amp was sittin' there, and he wanted to play that thing, and I hooked him up. And I started to walk back over to the counter to finish up some business, and I got about three steps before I realized that I was walking away from somebody who could play better than anybody I'd ever heard up to that time. I mean, he was already playing better than anybody I'd ever heard. I mean, better than any of them. [laughs] He was faster, cleaner, his intonation was perfect…I'll never forget it because I was never the same after that day.

Johnson blew through his audition and was immediately hired as the second member of the band. Bassist Bob Trenchard rounded out the power trio, and the group recorded its first demo in November 1969. However, before the band could cut its first single, Trenchard left to join the band Pall Rabbit (which would also go on to record with Sonobeat).

Trenchard was replaced by bassist and vocalist Jay Podolnick, and the band was ready to record its first official release for Sonobeat. The A side of its first single featured an original composition co-written with Sonosong lyricist Herman M. Nelson. "Re-Birth Day" was backed with "Memories Lost and Found" and gave Johnson a chance to show off his bourgeoning jazz-inflicted guitar style.

Today, the record is a highly sought-after collector's item, but at the time of release, it failed to make an impact with local reviewers or radio stations. For the next release, Bill and Rim decided the band needed some additional musical support.

They replaced Podolnick with bassist Jimmy Bullock. They also recruited singer and songwriter Bill Wilson, who had recorded a demo album for Sonosong Publishing. Vince brought in St. Edwards University musician Darrell Peal, and the band worked up some new material. Just as they were ready to cut a full-length album, Bill decided that a change of location from the Western Hills Drive studio was in order. Wanting a bigger space and a more removed environment, he decided to rent a vacant ranch near McDade, Texas, about thirty miles east of Austin.

Things did not go smoothly at the ranch. Prior to recording, a massive rainstorm soaked the land, rendering the dirt and gravel road leading to the ranch house unnavigable. The truck Bill used to transport the recording equipment got stuck in the mud, and everyone—the band members included—was needed to help push it out. Once they got the equipment to the ranch house, Bill and Rim prepared the consoles while the band set up in a large field outside. The plan was to capture the band with as "clean" a sound as possible; however, this proved to be more difficult than Bill and Rim expected. After burning through reel upon reel of half-inch tape over a three-day period, Bill, Rim and the band finally felt they had the basic tracks.

These tracks were then brought back to the Western Hills Drive studio for overdubs. Vocals, additional guitar and percussion parts and a series of jazzy between-song interludes and unorthodox studio experiments (one of which included the use of a Slinky attached to the ceiling with a microphone and piece of cardboard attached to the other end) completed the album, which Rim named *Perpetuum Mobile* and released under the band name "Mariani." As with previous Sonobeat albums, Bill Josey ordered one hundred promotional copies for distribution to major labels in hopes of procuring a deal.

Once again, Sonobeat was unable to replicate the success of the first Johnny Winter album. But once again, the label was successful at capturing an important moment in the earliest stages of a major artist's career. Though Mariani disbanded shortly after the completion of *Perpetuum Mobile*, Eric Johnson would go on to Guitar Hero status as one of the most highly acclaimed lead players of the 1980s and '90s. His second solo album, 1990's *Ah Via Musicom*, sold over one million copies, and in 2006, he was recognized in *Guitar Player* magazine as "one of the most respected guitarists on the planet." In 2008, a rare signed copy of one of the one hundred original *Perpetuum Mobile* albums was auctioned online for $2,850.

Sonobeat Records' consistent ability to find undiscovered talent underscores its role as a major contributor to the Austin music scene's unique formation. Unlike other major entertainment industry centers such as Los Angeles, Nashville, New York and Chicago, Austin did not have an abundance of major record labels, recording studios, publishing houses or A&R (artists and repertoire) types. Musicians did not flock to Austin in search of their big break. Instead, entrepreneurs such as Bill Josey scoured the clubs for talent, hoping to record an up-and-coming artist for free in exchange for being able to shop the rights to the master tape to a major label at a later date. The fact that they were not particularly successful in financial terms may have even helped Austin's cause; instead of becoming an industry behemoth, it remained an "underground" musician's town.

By establishing Sonobeat Records, Bill and Rim were ostensibly the only game in town, meaning they virtually had their pick of talented artists to record. Because even at that early stage there were so many talented musicians in Austin, the two music aficionados ended up recording many musicians who later went on to national prominence. The Sonobeat roster also helped to establish Austin's reputation as an emerging musical hotbed, one that would go on to attract both major artists and international acclaim in the decades to follow.

Blue Hole Sounds

Sonobeat's Latter Period

In June 1970, Rim Kelley married his longtime girlfriend and prepared for a move to Houston in order to attend law school. This left Bill Josey as the sole proprietor of Sonobeat Records, though Rim would return occasionally to help with engineering and mixing. Bill continued to operate Sonosong Publishing as well, pressing one hundred copies of Austin songwriter Roy Headrick's catalogue and sending them to record labels in Nashville. The Mariani single "Re-Birth Day" proved to be the only commercial Sonobeat release of 1970.

The Vulcan, which had always struggled to pay rent due to its inability to obtain a liquor license, closed in July. Not missing a beat, a group of Austin music figures including Eddie Wilson, Spencer Perskin, Jim Franklin, Mike Tolleson and Bobby Hedderman established the Armadillo World Headquarters on Barton Springs Road between First and Riverside only a month later.

Around this time, Bill shifted his focus from scouting artists for Sonobeat's roster to picking up custom recording work. One of the sessions he did later that year was with a band called Wildfire, which had recently relocated to Austin from Southern California. A power three-piece fronted by Randy Love (cousin of Beach Boys vocalist and songwriter Mike Love), the band had been brought out to Austin to play a party at the Hill on the Moon, the same ranch house inhabited by John Inmon, Layton DePenning, Donny Dolan and Leonard Arnold.

The band members immediately took to the laid-back vibe of the city and decided to stick around. Before long, they found out about Bill

Downtown Austin, 1976. *Photo courtesy of Larry D. Moore.*

and his studio and decided to hire him to record a demo. Though never released through Sonobeat Records, the recordings eventually resulted in the independent album *Smokin'*. The record helped Wildfire become one of the most popular rock bands in Austin at the time, regularly drawing large crowds at the Armadillo.[24]

In 1971, Bill reunited with some artists who had previously recorded under the Sonobeat label. He recorded a second Afro-Caravan album and attempted to shop it to Liberty Records, the same label that had purchased the group's first album, *Home Lost and Found*. However, this time the major label passed on the album. It remains unreleased to this day.

Josey also produced five songs for Fast Cotton, a heavier successor to the Sweetarts. Josey and bandleader Ernie Gammage had high hopes of creating Sonobeat's next "supergroup," but the band split up before a record could be released. Gammage moved to England shortly thereafter before returning to central Texas to form the band Plum Nelly.

In 1971, while in the midst of a recording project with a new group formed around singer/songwriter Bill Miller, Bill Josey and his wife divorced. The separation marked the end of the home studio on Western Hills Drive, and Josey moved his operations to a rental space on the ground floor of the KVET building on North Lamar. Josey finished the sessions with

Miller, which resulted in the album *Cold Sun*, but once again his attempts at selling the album to a major label fell short. The *Cold Sun* album remained unreleased until the Dallas-based psychedelic indie label Rockedelic issued a few hundred copies in 1989.

During the time period shortly following the divorce, Bill Josey took on an increasing amount of custom recording work, as opposed to scouting for talent to record and release (or pitch to major labels) under the Sonobeat brand. The only official Sonobeat releases of '71 were two gospel singles by the Royal Lights Singers, a traditional folk ensemble that played one of the earliest Kerville Folk Festivals and continues to perform in Austin some forty-two years later. The following year followed the same trend, with Josey working almost exclusively as a producer-for-hire.

By this time, the progressive country movement had started to take shape in Austin, and many of the musicians who cut their teeth recording for Sonobeat were now on their way to national prominence. "Outlaw" singer/songwriters and cosmic cowboys such as Willie Nelson, Jerry Jeff Walker and Michael Martin Murphy had all settled in Austin by around this time, and former Sonobeat-affiliated musicians Gary P. Nunn and John Inmon would soon join Bob Livingston and Mike McGeary to form Walker's longtime backing band, the Lost Gonzo Band. Former Lavender Hill Express member Rusty Wier would go on to sign a deal to ABC Records, releasing his debut, *Stoned, Slow, Rugged*, in 1974. Leonard Arnold recalls:

> *Everybody that was playing in those bands, including the Lavender Hill and Genesee and all those bands we went through; everybody in those bands eventually went to work with those guys* [in the progressive country movement]. *When those guys moved to town, everybody in that group of people I was hanging with were thinking country or trying to switch to it. In fact, Don Henley was one of those guys, and you know what he did. We were all playing rock, and he was bringing in the Dillards to listen to.* [laughs] *Don Henley was in a group in* [North] *Texas called Felicity,*[25] *and they were another band that came to Austin pretty regularly and packed the house every time.*

Another era in Austin music had begun.

After a couple years spent mostly doing recording work for hire, Bill Josey began 1973 with renewed determination to find undiscovered talent for the Sonobeat label. After a recording session with Michele Murphy, the Austin singer/songwriter brought his attention to a hardly used church building in the small community of Liberty Hill, located in the Hill Country thirty-five miles northwest of Austin. In August '73, Bill Sr. moved onto the property and refurbished the building with recording equipment, christening the new studio Blue Hole Sounds.

With help from Leander resident and singer/songwriter Tom Penick, Josey built the studio and began to try to drum up business around Austin.

By early 1975, Bill was preparing to release the first Sonobeat single in over two years, a folk single by Round Rock singer/songwriter Arma Harper titled "Just One Too Many Times." But just as his recording enterprise was getting back on track, Bill began to experience fatigue and physical discomfort. The problems persisted, and he went to see a doctor.

Bill was diagnosed with lymphoma carcinoma, a malignant cancer that preys on the circulatory system. Surgery was his only option. Jack Josey remembers:

> *Right after my dad underwent cancer surgery in 1975, I moved to Liberty Hill to take care of him. As it turned out, he did more for me than I did for him. I was away during the day at work in Georgetown and at classes at UT in Austin. I moved in with him more to keep him company. When I arrived at his mobile home in the evening, he would either have supper ready for both of us or we'd drive to the café in downtown Liberty Hill, where he knew everyone's name—waitresses and patrons alike. While staying with him, he encouraged me to apply for a job as a radio announcer at KGTN in nearby Georgetown, which I did, and landed a morning on-air shift. Dad took a practical approach on doing good things with our lives. Even though he was recuperating from surgery, he'd get up early in the morning, start my car and clean my car windows before I left for the early morning shift at KGTN. It was his way of showing me he cared about me without having to say the words "I love you."*

With the help of his younger son Jack, Bill was able to release the "Just One Too Many Times" single, as well as the David Flack Quorum jazz album *Mindbender*, recorded six years earlier. The final Sonobeat release appeared in the spring of 1976, with the Jeannine Hoke single "Your Touch Is Like a Whisper," backed with "Let's Get to Houston Today." Slowed down by chemotherapy, Bill Josey was increasingly unable to produce records. Jack remembers:

> *In June 1976, Dad threw a big university graduation party under the live oak trees next to the rock church for my older sister, Deb. In July, he*

The David Flack Quorum's *Mindbender*, one of only two official Sonobeat full-length album releases. *Courtesy of Sonobeat Historical Archives.*

walked my younger sister, Jan, down the aisle for her wedding in Austin. A day or two after the wedding, Dad asked me to drive him to the Veterans Administration Hospital in Temple. He wanted to check himself in. He was too weak to go on. Deb and I hoped that the doctors at the VA Hospital would be able to cure Dad with the newest thing we had read about: Laetrile. We took articles about Laetrile with us to the VA Hospital and gave them to the doctors. Whether they read them or not, we'll never know. I drove several times a week to Temple to visit Dad at the hospital. In August, I took him for one last drive to Liberty Hill to see his studio in the old rock church. He was calm with a smile on his face as we drove through the back roads from Temple to Liberty Hill. Without the ability to record demos for musicians on a regular basis and therefore make money during his illness, Dad was financially strapped the last couple of years of his life. An unbearably painful moment I witnessed was when he asked me to wheel him through the color-coded hallways of the VA Hospital to a pay phone. I stood back as he sat in the wheelchair beneath the phone attached to the wall, slowly reaching up and inserting coins. He called people who had loaned him money, and I could hear him telling each of them, "I'm going to be out of here soon and will pay you back."

Bill Josey Sr. died on September 28, 1976. His funeral was held a few days later, with a handful of family and friends in attendance. He was buried in the only suit he owned—a blue polyester leisure suit his children had given him a few years earlier.

Sonobeat's Impact on the Austin Music Scene

The same year that Bill Josey Sr. succumbed to lymphoma carcinoma, a new television show premiered nationally on PBS. The show was titled *Austin City Limits* and was created to celebrate the music of the Lone Star State. The following year, the producers made Gary P. Nunn's now-iconic "London Homesick Blues" the show's theme song, cued while the end credits rolled after each week's performance. The former keyboard player for the Lavender Hill Express had gone on to create one of the quintessential anthems of Texas music.

Shortly after Bill Josey Sr. passed away, Austin music journalist and historian Doug Hanners wrote a profile in his magazine, *Don't Fade Away*, chronicling the label's contribution to Austin music. The article emphasized the label's eclecticism and singled out KAZZ as the voice of the "rapidly growing Austin music scene" of the mid-1960s. Hanners recalls how the idea for the article came about when he was working at Discount Records across Guadalupe Street from the Texas Union:

> *I was in the music business in Austin at a record shop, and I collected records and got interested a lot of the older stuff around Austin. So I did this magazine, and it had a lot of different articles in the issues that I did, and Sonobeat was one of them 'cause it was a big part of Austin's musical history. I got to know Bill Josey. He was ill then and was on his way out, but he was still very helpful, and I talked to him and interviewed him a lot. He was a nice guy, very helpful. Quite an older gentleman, but he was*

South Congress Avenue, Austin, Texas. *Photo courtesy of Justin Jensen.*

very helpful to everything that I was trying to do. Bill was basically on his deathbed; I think he died about six months after I finished the interview. But he was a very helpful, very nice guy. This was way before record shows were going on. I was just collecting a lot of the records and information about the '50s and '60s days in Texas and around Austin, and Sonobeat was a big part of it. So I eventually decided to do a story just on them because they were such a huge part of the Austin music scene in those days. Back in the '60s there weren't many record labels for the fledgling music scene in Austin. And Sonobeat provided that, and they had some major

labels that worked with them. They put out the Johnny Winter album that Imperial Records picked up, and that was basically his entry to the national music scene. There were others from Sonobeat, but his was probably the biggest because he got such huge publicity and went on to be very successful and was one of the early guitar zens of Texas and Austin.

Because Sonobeat was one of the only independent record labels operating out of Austin in the late 1960s, Bill Josey and Rim Kelley essentially had their pick of some of Austin's top musical talent. Keeping that in mind, it is no surprise that so many of the musicians associated with Sonobeat went on to have successful careers in the music industry and are rightly recognized as influential figures in the history of the Austin music scene.

Not Fade Away magazine, featuring Sonobeat Records, 1977. *Courtesy of Doug Hanners.*

Sonobeat's roster had included some of the most popular local acts in a city that would soon explode into the national spotlight. Yet to this day, there remains little documentation of Sonobeat's story. Despite the scarcity of information about Sonobeat, the label's twenty-six commercial releases have survived to become extremely rare collectors' items, pursued by collectors on both sides of the Atlantic. An offhand search on eBay at the time of this writing yields the Conqueroos' "1 to 3/I've Got Time" single listed for $125; a copy of the David Flack Quorum's *Mindbender* LP runs for $200.

Each of the original Sonobeat releases, along with numerous artifacts and documents related to the label, have been preserved by the Josey family. According to Jack Josey:

> *The tapes are in sealed waterproof containers in climate-controlled storage in the Austin area. We originally recovered the tapes from Liberty Hill right after my father died in the autumn of 1976. Believe it or not, they were crammed into cardboard boxes in my father's station wagon along with various other Sonobeat material. We don't know who put them in the car—it wasn't my father because he was in the VA hospital until his death. My brother-in-law and I towed the car back to Austin, where we then stored the tapes on the second unused floor of my elderly cousin's house in West Austin where we knew no one ever ventured. They sat there for ten years before I retrieved them and took them to my house in Georgetown. And they sat another fifteen years in a closet until Bill and I decided to put together the Sonobeat website in 2004. At that time, I started digitizing short audio clips for the site. Then in 2008, I took on the task of digitizing every tape in the Sonobeat library. To do that, I had to repair many of the tapes because the splicing tape had deteriorated and started falling apart between tracks on the tapes. There are two copies of the digitized tapes on two separate hard drives at separate locations. Sonobeat documents and artifacts are divided up among my siblings.*

Though only two Sonobeat albums broke through to national release, the label's influence on the Austin music scene is both widespread and widely overlooked. Sonobeat Records played a major role in developing the bedrock of Austin musicians that were already in town when the progressive country movement took hold. Jack Josey notes:

> *I believe Sonobeat was a key ingredient to the creation of the Austin Music Scene. If Sonobeat had never existed and never recorded the talented musicians it did, I doubt the Austin music scene would be at the level it's at today. My father and brother were not looking for fame. In fact, my father was not famous while living, and today he's famous only among avid fans and historians of Austin music from the '60s and '70s. My father and brother were just doing what they wanted to do—record music in Austin.*

John Inmon adds:

> *It was more or less a hobby for Bill [Sr.]. He wasn't trying to get rich off of this stuff; he was just a lover the music and of the technology. That was his big thing. And the disc jockeys loved the music, and they loved being part of the scene, and they were local stars, too. They could help the bands and the bands could help them and the records helped everybody, so it was a pretty cool deal for everybody.*

Tommy Taylor remembers:

> *There was a lot of music going on, and Josey saw that. He saw Vince Mariani as a drummer and put out a stereo single of two drum solos. That's a pretty unusual approach. [laughs] It's not really marketable in a certain way; it's kind of a strange thing to do. But Vince was an amazing drummer, and to see that and recognize it and to want to put that out there was certainly admirable. It seemed like every group in Austin that was anybody was gonna end up putting something out on Sonobeat. And a lot of people did.*

In the years shortly following Sonobeat's peak period of operation, outlaw country became wildly popular as a rock-and-roll-influenced alternative to the Nashville sound. Willie Nelson, Waylon Jennings, Kris Kristofferson, Townes Van Zandt and Billy Joe Shaver were some of the names most closely associated with the subgenre, all of whom shared ties to Texas.

Other artists such as Jerry Jeff Walker, Guy Clark, Michael Martin Murphy, B.W. Stevenson, Willis Alan Ramsay and Steve Fromholz based careers out of Austin that were not as overtly iconoclastic, yet they, too, abandoned many of the industry conventions of Nashville and Los Angeles. Preferring the laid-back environment of 1970s Austin, they ended up collaborating with many of the musicians who had cut their teeth recording for Sonobeat Records. John Inmon recalls:

> *There was a little scene that supported original music, then there was a music scene in the early '70s that attracted the actual record industry. And then there was the blues thing in the '80s that really put Austin on the map. And it's been an iconic town ever since then. But it really took a long time for it to build to that. There's no specific point…everything just sort of blended together, like a watercolor painting. Everything just sort of runs*

together, and that's how these events happened. If I had to say something was like the magic wand, it was when everybody was really emphasizing original music. And Willie and Michael Martin Murphy came to town and attracted the record industry. And the record industry was loaded. They had so much dough it was pathetic. So they were sending guys out all over the country, wherever the action was. Well, Austin was hot as a pistol at that point. They were coming in and signing acts and all that kind of stuff.

Instead of building a reputation as a powerful cutthroat industry city, Austin built a name for itself as a naturally laid-back town that was home to many talented musicians and receptive audiences. The city's reputation was further cemented with the success of *Austin City Limits*. New music venues such as the Armadillo Headquarters, Antone's and Liberty Lunch proved to be launching pads for new artists such as Joe Ely and Stevie Ray Vaughan, and in 1978, the Pecan Street Festival was established, helping to revitalize the Sixth Street district.

In the 1980s and '90s, Austin's Sixth Street became a world-renowned live music hub of its own. In 1987, the South by Southwest music conference was established, ensuring that Austin would remain a major musical center for decades to come.

The Sweetarts reunion show, 2011. *Photo courtesy of Ernie Gammage.*

Today, the Sonobeat legacy is carried on mostly by the Josey family and the musicians and music fans familiar with the label. All twenty-six commercial Sonobeat releases have been preserved by the Josey family; additional copies can be found among the archives at the Dolph Briscoe Center for American History at the University of Texas in Austin.

With all of the famous musicians and music-related events that have taken place in Austin over the last few decades, it is worthwhile to recognize the key role played by Sonobeat Records in the early stages of the Austin music scene. Bill Josey and Rim Kelley, and all the musicians who recorded with Sonobeat, played an important part in making Austin the great music town it has become today.

Though much of the music and many of the events that occurred in Austin during this time period have been largely overlooked, they have not been forgotten. They remain as hazy memories in the minds of those who were there and in the recorded material passed down to the generations beyond.

Success is measured in many ways, but in the record business at least, the music speaks for itself.

—*Doug Hanners,* Not Fade Away *magazine, 1977*

Notes

A Brief History of Music in Austin Up to the 1960s

1. Dobie, like Lomax, played a major role in popularizing the image of the American cowboy. A University of Texas English professor, folklorist and writer, Dobie published many articles and books about Texas history and life on the open range, including titles such as *A Vaquero of the Brush Country*, *Coronado's Children* and *The Longhorns*.
2. The second chapter of Barry Shank's 1994 publication *Dissonant Identities: The Rock n' Roll Scene in Austin, Texas*, provides a good summary of the earliest period of Austin's musical heritage while arguing that the "performance of identity" witnessed in the singing cowboy has maintained a presence in Austin music and culture that endures to the present day.
3. Williams, arguably the most iconic country singer who ever lived, made his final public performance in December 1952 at the Skyline Club, one such honky-tonk located on the old Dallas Highway (now Lamar Boulevard) just north of the Austin City Limits.
4. For more on this formative period in Austin's cultural history, see Scott Conn's 2008 documentary, *Dirt Road to Psychedelia*.
5. Between 1924 and 1973, the *Austin American* published on weekday mornings, while the *Austin Statesman* served as the afternoon paper. The weekend edition, in which this article appeared, was combined as the *American-Statesman*.

6. Johnson's support of the civil rights movement, including the signing of the Civil Rights Act in 1964, proved to be one of the lasting achievements of his legacy. Unfortunately, so did the rapid *escalation* of the war in Vietnam.

7. A decade and a half later, it would be renovated and transformed into one of the most revered venues in Austin's history, the Armadillo World Headquarters.

8. Paul Drummond's *Eye Mind: The Saga of Roky Erickson and the 13th Floor Elevators* (Process Media, 2007) provides an excellent detailed account of the legendary band's tumultuous career.

9. Franklin soon became a well-known figure in Austin, both for his iconic poster art and album covers as well as his colorful personality. After the Vulcan Gas Company closed in 1970, Franklin moved into the Armadillo World Headquarters, serving as house artist, booking agent and emcee. He is probably most famous for his numerous paintings and drawings featuring armadillos, which became a sort of symbol for the youth counterculture movement in Texas and provided the World Headquarters with its namesake.

AUSTIN RADIO AND KAZZ-FM

10. Today, "Rim" once again goes by Bill Josey; however, for the sake of this book, he will be referred to as Rim Kelley except for when using present-day interview quotations.

A PICTURE OF ME

11. In fact, almost all records, including twelve-inch LPs, were released in mono until the mid- to late 1960s, when they were largely phased out by high-fidelity stereo recordings.

12. Soon, KAZZ would transform into KOKE-FM, which would gain regional fame as the first radio station to regularly program southern rock alongside the rock-inflicted "progressive country" music of Willie Nelson, Jerry Jeff Walker and Michael Martin Murphy. In 1974, *Billboard* magazine singled out KOKE-FM as the most innovative radio station in the United States.

13. Shelton would go on to build a successful career in the underground comics industry as the creator of *The Fabulous Furry Freak Brothers*, a light-

hearted series based on a trio of stumbling hippies and their run-ins with the police and the rest of society.

14. Franklin would later design album covers by Shiva's Headband, Freddie King and Commander Cody and his Lost Planet Airmen.

15. The base was transformed into Austin-Bergstrom International Airport and opened to the public on May 23, 1999.

16. James Polk holds down a Monday night residency at the Continental Club Gallery on South Congress Avenue in Austin to the present day.

Mean Town Blues

17. Shannon would later go on to further fame as bassist for Stevie Ray Vaughan's Double Trouble.

18. The article even gives honorable mention to two future Texas songwriting legends: Townes Van Zandt and Guy Clark. Van Zandt's debut album, *For the Sake of the Song*, had come out a month earlier. Clark was yet to release a record.

19. In the mid-1970s, Hanners established *Not Fade Away*, a magazine dedicated to Austin's music history. The magazine ran a profile of Sonobeat Records in 1977.

20. An example of Pryor's humor: on Thanksgiving Day 1952, Austin launched its first local television broadcast, covering the UT–Texas A&M football game on KTBC. The first image broadcast, prior to the game, was Cactus's bald head. His first words: "What, were you expecting hair?"

21. Wier's 1975 song "Don't It Make You Wanna Dance" would become a regional hit, leading to cover versions by artists such as Chris Le Doux, Jerry Jeff Walker and Barbara Mandrell. In 1980, Wier struck gold when a version by Bonnie Raitt was included on the double platinum–selling soundtrack for *Urban Cowboy*.

Home Lost and Found

22. During this time period, foldout covers, with their four full-cover production plates, were much more costly to produce and were generally reserved for records that would receive heavy promotion from the label.

23. A close look at the Sonobeat discography shows that Rim was given producer credit for most of the rock releases, while Bill produced more of

the jazz/country/folk music releases. This underscores how Sonobeat was able to have a very eclectic roster while still developing and maintaining a distinct collective style.

BLUE HOLE SOUNDS

24. Wildfire broke up in 1972 but reunited in the last decade. The band released a digitally re-mastered CD version of *Smokin'* in 2006.
25. Felicity had started out as Henley's high school band, originally called the Four Speeds, in Gilmer, Texas, in the mid-1960s. The members caught the attention of country singer Kenny Rodgers, who moved the band out to Los Angeles in 1970. Shortly thereafter, Henley joined the Eagles, one of the most popular recording artists in the history of the music business.

Works Cited

Arnold, Leonard. Interview with author, August 12, 2013.

Barkley, M.S. *History of Travis County and Austin 1839–1899*. Austin, TX: Austin Printing Company, 1963.

Bishop, C., and R.L. Schroeter. *Austin American-Statesman*. Handbook of Texas Online. http://www.tshaonline.org/handbook/online/articles/eeal1 (accessed September 30, 2013).

"The Broken Spoke Legend." Broken Spoke website. http://www.brokenspokeaustintx.com/legend.htm (accessed September 23, 2013).

Campi, R. (composer). *Civil Disobedience*. Performed by R. Campi. Austin, TX: United States of America, 1968.

Capstar Broadcasting Partners, Inc. *Capstar Broadcasting Partners to Acquire Radio Stations KASE-FM and KVET-AM/FM*. December 22, 1977. PR Newswire. http://www.prnewswire.com/news-releases/capstar-broadcasting-partners-to-acquire-radio-stations-kase-fm-and-kvet-amfm-77949782.html (accessed September 9, 2013).

Cash Box Magazine. Record Reviews. October 7, 1967; June 20, 1968.

Chadbourne, E. *Bach Yen Artist Biography*. Allmusic. http://www.allmusic. com/artist/bach-yen-mn0001306714/biography (accessed September 23, 2013).

Chesnut, J. *Jim Chesnut Biography*. 2012. Jim Chesnut artist website. http:// www.chesnutproductions.com (accessed September 23, 2013).

City of Austin. *Austin: Live Music Capital of the World*. Austin Convention & Visitors Bureau website. http://www.austintexas.org (accessed September 23, 2013).

Corcoran, M. "Little Indie Label Domino Laid Down Austin Sounds Before Scene's Heyday." *Austin American-Statesman*, June 4, 2010.

DePenning, Layton. Interview with author, October 7, 2012.

Drummond, P. *Eye Mind: The Saga of Roky Erickson and the 13th Floor Elevators, the Pioneers of Psychedelic Sound*. Los Angeles: Process Media, 2007.

Duane, F. *HemisFair '68*. Handbook of Texas Online. http://www.tshaonline. org/handbook/online/articles/lkh01 (accessed September 25, 2013).

Eliot, M. *To the Limit: the Untold Story of the Eagles*. Cambridge, MA: Da Capo Press, 2004.

Emmis Austin Radio Broadcasting Company, Lp. *KLBJ: The Story of Austin Radio*. 2003. KLBJ FM website. http://klbjfm.dvdfuture.com/history.php (accessed September 9, 2013).

Franklin, Jim. Interview with author, July 26, 2013.

Gammage, Ernie. Interview with author, October 10, 2012.

Gandara, R. "Cactus Pryor, Austin's Original Funnyman, Dies at 88." *Austin American-Statemsan*, August 30, 2011.

Goodwin, D.K. *Lyndon Johnson and the American Dream*. New York: Haper & Row, 1976.

Greisman, M. *The Thingies: from Topeka to Miami to Austin!* 1998. Cicadelic Records website. http://www.cicadelic.com/thingies.htm (accessed September 23, 2013).

Guinn, Ed. XE "Conqueroo" Interview with author, August 26, 2013.

Hall, C. "KAZZ Specializes in Not Specializing." *Billboard,* June 21, 1965.

Hanners, D. "Sonobeat Records: Austin in the 1960s." *Not Fade Away*, 1977.

Hanners, Doug. Interview with author, August 8, 2013.

Hendrickson, P. "Janis Joplin: A Cry Cutting Through Time." *Washington Post*, May 5, 1998.

Inmon, John. Interview with author, July 26, 2013.

————. John Inmon Artist website. http://johninmon.com (accessed September 23, 2013).

James-Reed, M.O. *Music in Austin, 1900–1956.* Austin, TX: Von Boeckmann-Jones Company, 1957 .

Joseph, Y. (composer). Stick-To-It-Ive-Ness. Performed by J.P. Brothers. Austin, TX: United States of America, 1969.

Josey, Bill, Jr. Interview with author, October 20, 2012.

Josey, Bill, Jr., and Jack Josey. "Sonobeat: The Beginning of the Austin Music Scene." 2004–2013. http://sonobeatrecords.com (accessed 2013).

Josey, Bill, Sr. Interview with Doug Hanners, August 31, 1976.

Josey, Jack. Interview with author, August 9, 2013.

Karnow, S. *Vietnam: A History.* Revised ed. New York: Penguin, 1997.

King, Wali. Interview with author, August 12, 2013.

KLRU-TV, PBS Austin. "History of ACL." 2012. Austin City Limits website. http://acltv.com/history-of-acl (accessed September 19, 2013).

Lavergne, G.M. *A Sniper in the Tower: The Charles Whitman Murders.* Denton: University of North Texas Press, 1997.

Leslie, J. "On Tackling Odd Meters: Eric Johnson." *Guitar Player*, August 2006.

Lundborg, P. "Cold Sun: Austin's Lost Psychedelic Visionaries." 2011. Lysergia website. http://www.lysergia.com/LamaWorkshop/lamaColdSun.htm (accessed September 20, 2013).

McMurtry, C. "Disbelief, Horror Shroud Capital City." *Austin American-Statesman*, November 23. 1963, 7.

Moser, M. "Hank, Harry, and Jesse James: Steel Player Jimmy Grabowske Saw It All." *Austin Chronicle*, October 5, 2007

O'Neal, B. *Tex Ritter: America's Most Beloved Cowboy.* Fort Worth, TX: Eakin Press, 1998.

Pinson, M. "Eric Johnson: In Full Bloom." August 6, 2008. MusicPlayers. com. http://musicplayers.com (accessed September 23, 2013).

Reid, J. *The Improbable Rise of Redneck Rock.* New ed. Austin: University of Texas Press, 2004.

Rothenbuhler, E. "Radio Redefines Itself, 1947–1962." In *Radio Reader: Essays in the Cultural History of Radio*, edited by M. Hilmes and J. Loviglio. London: Routledge, 2001.

Seida, L. "Rusty Wier Artist Biography." Allmusic website. http://www. allmusic.com/artist/rusty-wier-mn0000209722/biography (accessed September 23, 2013).

Sepulvedo, L., and J. Brooks. "Texas. *Rolling Stone*, December 6, 1968, 16–17.

Simon, C.L. "Vulcan Gas Company." Handbook of Texas Online. http://www.tshaonline.org/handbook/online/articles/xdv01 (accessed September 29, 2013).

Slate, J.H. *Lost Austin.* Charleston, SC: Arcadia Publishing, 2012.

Stimeling, T.D. *Cosmic Cowboys and New Hicks: The Countercultural Sounds of Austin's Progressive Country Music Scene.* Oxford, UK: Oxford University Press, 2011.

Sullivan, M.L. *Raisin' Cain: The Wild and Raucous Story of Johnny Winter.* Milwaukee, WI: Backbeat Books, 2010.

Taylor, Tommy. Interview with author, September 27, 2013.

"Twink Records Biography." Twink Records website. http://www.twinkrecords.com/bio.htm (accessed September 19, 2013).

U.S. Census Bureau and the City of Austin. "City of Austin Population History: 1840 to 2013." City of Austin official website. http://www.austintexas.gov/sites/default/files/files/Planning/Demographics/population_history_pub.pdf (accessed September 23, 2013).

U.S. Department of Commerce. "State and County Quick Facts: Austin, Texas." United States Census Bureau. http://quickfacts.census.gov/qfd/states/48/4805000.html (accessed September 23, 2013).

Wheat, J. "Armadillo World Headquarters." Handbook of Texas Online. http://www.tshaonline.org/handbook/online/articles/xda01 (accessed September 29, 2013).

Whitefield, P. "The Sweetarts Discography." Scarlet Dukes website. http://www.scarletdukes.com/st/discography.html#som (accessed September 26, 2013).

Wildfire. "History: Texas." 2007. Wildfire website. http://www.wildfire-smokin.com/history4.html (accessed September 29, 2013).

Index

About the Author

R icky Stein is a writer and musician from Austin, Texas. After graduating from McCallum High School in 2002, he pursued a career as a singer/songwriter in the Live Music Capital, performing regularly at the Hole in the Wall, the Saxon Pub and the Continental Club. In 2004, he began writing for the *West Austin News*, which led to additional writing opportunities at the *Round Rock Leader* and the *Austin American-Statesman*. While completing his degree in American studies at the University of Texas, Stein contributed weekly articles to the *Daily Texan. Sonobeat Records: Pioneering the Austin Sound in the '60s* is his first book.

Photo by Emily Morganti.